A dog lies in the shade in the summer time.

He lies in the sun during the winter.

Thirty years of exploration into biology, physics and human nature have brought me to the realization that humanity has, itself, forged the sword that is potentially responsible for piercing its own heart.

We have corralled ourselves with laws and codes that, while written to protect us, are also keeping us from evolving at the pace necessary to keep up with global change and population explosion. This is much like a barn built to protect horses from the cold. By an act of fate it catches on fire and traps them inside to burn to death. Due to global change and increasing population, our barn is burning. Our laws and codes have become barriers that won't let us escape the burning barn fast enough to survive. The future will bring humanity extreme hardship unless we can bypass certain laws and codes in designated areas in order to experiment with new and more logical ways of living in our physical environment.

In the 1940's, New Mexico designated several thousand acres of land for testing weapons of nuclear destruction. There, scientiests dropped an atomic bomb. Many codes, and environmental standards were put aside for this endeavor in the name of defense from our enemies. Can't we now take this same bold step to designate both acreage and legislation in every state to explore methods of sustainable life on this planet? The evolution of sustainable living methods must be allowed a "test site", free from the crippling restraints of laws, codes and basic human encumbrances, in the name of defense...
from our own failing methods of living.

This book has been written to explain a theory of how buildings can be made comforable without centralized utilities or use of fuel. In it I also present an application of the theory, the Earthship, which I've been developing for the past three decades. May these ideas lead you to discover a lighter and more connected way of living on the Earth.

Michael Reynolds

ISBN 0-9626767-4-8

First Printing August 2000
SOLAR SURVIVAL PRESS
P.O. Box 1041
Taos, New Mexico, 87571
www.earthship.org
biotecture@earthship.org
earthshipbiotecture.com
ph 505 751 0462
fax 505 751 1005

COMFORT

in any climate

Shelter

comfort in any climate

Capture a space that offers comfort to the human body throughout the storms and you have shelter. Shelter has evolved, over the centuries, from basic protection to complex interior environments supported by waning fossil fuels, nuclear fuels, and elaborate infrastructures

People used caves for shelter in the early days of humanity. This worked well when there were very few people on the planet. As population grew, other methods of shelter were needed. People made shelter from animal skins and tree poles. As numbers of people grew and numbers of animals decreased, still other methods of shelter evolved. Later, people made shelters from logs and then chopped up more logs to heat them. Still the numbers of people grew while the number of trees decreased. People now make shelter from framed lumber (a more efficient use of trees). They use various fuel sources for temperature control, but the numbers of people continue to grow and the numbers of trees and sources of fuel continue to decrease.

As modern day conditions with both people and planet change around us, it is becoming necessary to reassess how we conceive of and manifest shelter.

Above - Thermal mass shelter that encounters the natural phenomena of the Earth

Temperature control was introduced in shelters as humanity evolved and grew more aware of comfort. Comfortable temperature was achieved by the use of some form of fire for warming. In recent decades, cooling systems have evolved that also use some form of fire for energy to create the cool temperature. As temperature control became more desired and fuel for fire became more precious, insulation emerged as a factor of newer shelters. Insulation traps the temperature that is created inside the shelter. In modern times, millions of humans use some form of fire for both cooling and heating their often poorly insulated shelters. The problem is that **the creation and delivery of fire has become so costly to both humans and the Earth that the end of available fire is in sight.**

To meet our growing needs for inexpensive fuel to heat and cool our homes; efforts have been made to supplement fossil fuel use with nuclear source fuels. Any form of centralized energy production results in delivery through wires and pipes, and this is a detriment to the quality of life on Earth. Even if centralized energy were produced in a harmless way, which may be possible using hydrogen, **the delivery web is consuming us.** The ever increasing webs of wires and pipes, both above and below ground, are dangerous, unhealthy, ugly and expensive. Another downside of centralized energy production methods for controlling temperature in human shelters is dependency on the bureaucratic, political, and corporate giants that create and deliver the energy. These "giants" sometimes have a devastating effect on humanity themselves. And last there is the price (in money) that humans must forever pay for the manufacture and delivery of energy for maintaining a comfortable temperature in their shelter. This is felt in monthly expenses and taxes.

There are many reasons for pursuing shelter that is independent of conventional utility systems.

Shelter could be an effortless function of the natural processes of the planet but it is presently a struggle between people and planet resulting in serious stress to both.

All current methods of centralized energy production are detrimental to the quality of biological life due to their devastating environmental effects.

*"Heatng, cooling and lighting the world's built structures sucks up roughly one third of the massive flows of energy used by modern societies." **

Hundreds of people a year die in their homes from extreme heat or extreme cold due to failing utilities or inability to pay utility bills.

* POWER SURGE
by Christopher Flavin and Nicholas Lenssen

Present day human life has "static shelter" that is dependent on life support systems running to and from individual units. This is like an invalid on life support systems in a hospital. The future must bring housing units that are of the nature of the earth. These dwellings must dynamically "be" their systems.

A tree doesn't need a support system - it is a system.

For a system not to be static, it must be a contribution to the world around it. There must be encounter and exchange between a system and other systems in order to be part of the overall system - the universe.

That which contributes to its surroundings in the world at large is constantly reinforcing the strength of its own existence.

Presently both people and planet pay dearly for production and delivery of energy to maintain comfort in todays static shelter. Shelter of the future must be inherently capable of both collecting and storing appropriate temperature for human comfort in addition to providing protection from the elements. Human shelter must be redefined to become more integral with the natural processes of the Earth to achieve this. We must ultimately eliminate the manufacture and delivery of large amounts of energy to each individual shelter all over the Earth.

The shelter of the future will embody energy.

North side of a shelter that embodies energy in the Greater World Community in Taos, New Mexico

Mass and Insulation

comfort in any climate

Insulation

In recent years we have recognized the fact that insulation can help keep temperature in a shelter. Insulation, however, neither collects nor stores temperature. It simply blocks the passage of temperature from inside to out and visa versa. Good insulation has millions of tiny air spaces. The presence of air spaces tends to slow up the movement of temperature by causing it to pass from air space to air space as opposed to moving easily through unobstructed dense mass. Insulation acts as a blockade for temperature - not allowing it to enter or pass through.

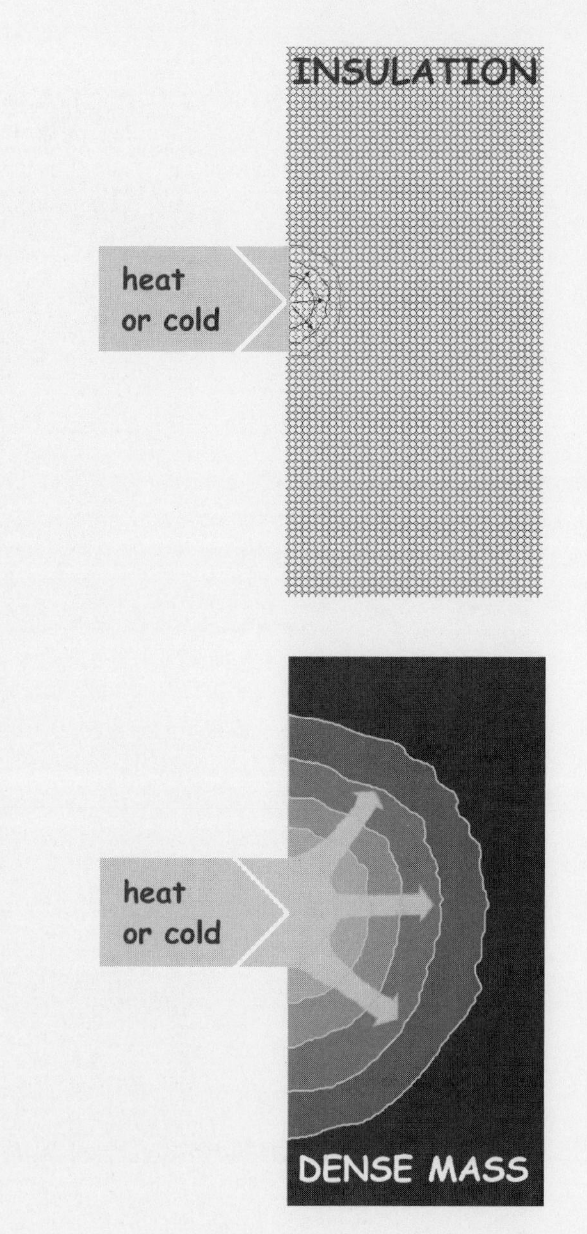

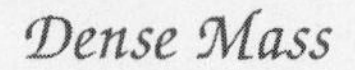

Dense Mass

Dense mass, also called thermal mass, absorbs and stores temperature much like a battery stores electricity. Examples of dense mass are stone, water, compacted earth, and concrete. **There is a major difference between mass and insulation.** Dense means the absence of voids or air spaces. The more dense the mass, the more temperature it holds. This density acts as a conduit for temperature allowing it to travel into the mass and be contained there.

An ideal wall would have both mass and insulation.

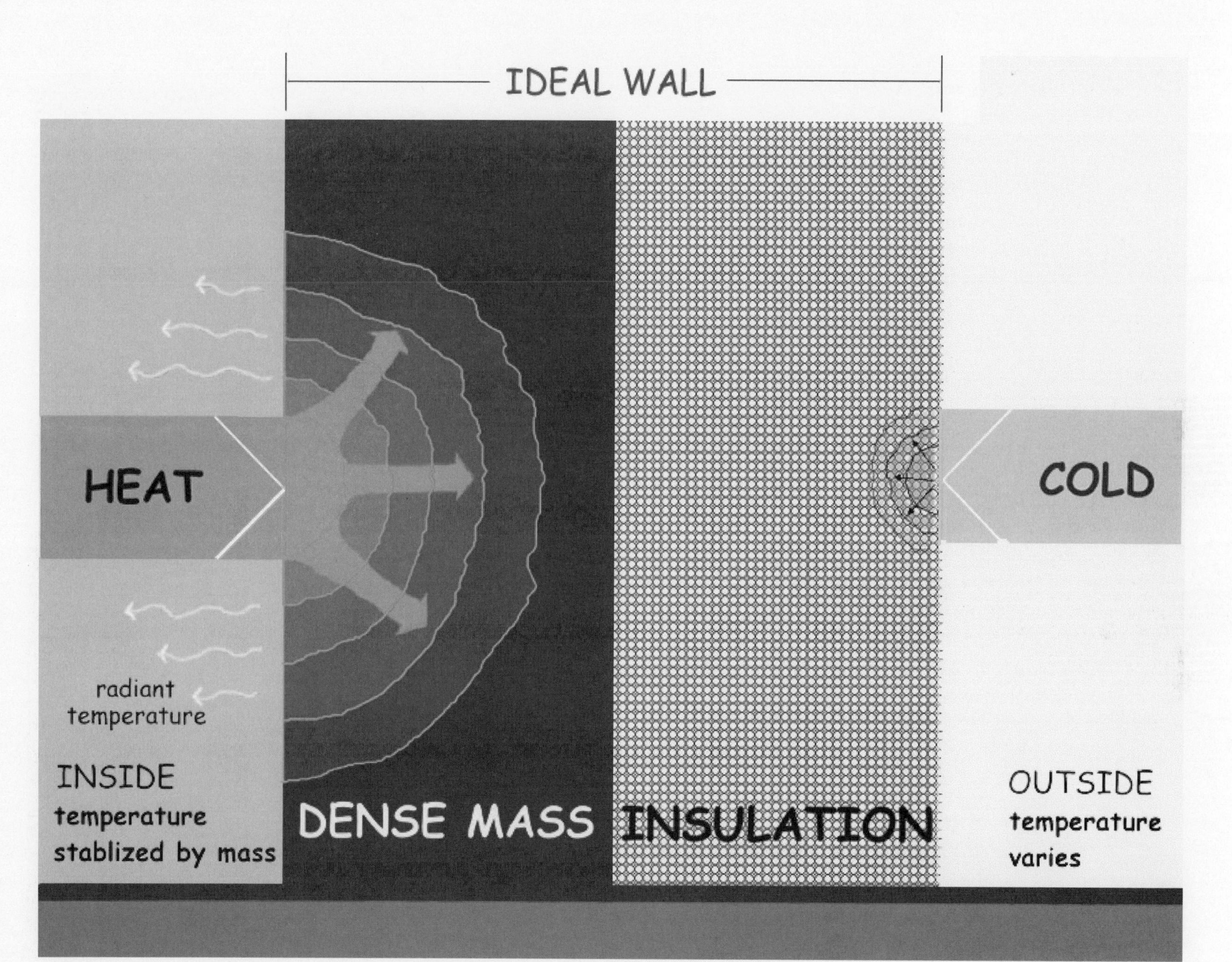

IDEAL WALL
HEAT
COLD
radiant
temperature
INSIDE
temperature
stablized by mass
DENSE MASS
INSULATION
OUTSIDE
temperature
varies

An Ideal Wall

Temperature can transform thermal mass from warm to cool or cool to warm while it has little effect on insulation. The perfect wall for a shelter that embodies energy would incorporate both mass and insulation. Thermal mass would be on the inside to initially "capture" the desired temperature from any source. Insulation would occur on the outside to keep the desired interior temperature from escaping and to separate it from outside temperature. Temperature stored in the interior dense mass stabilizes the temperature of the living space creating comfort in that space.

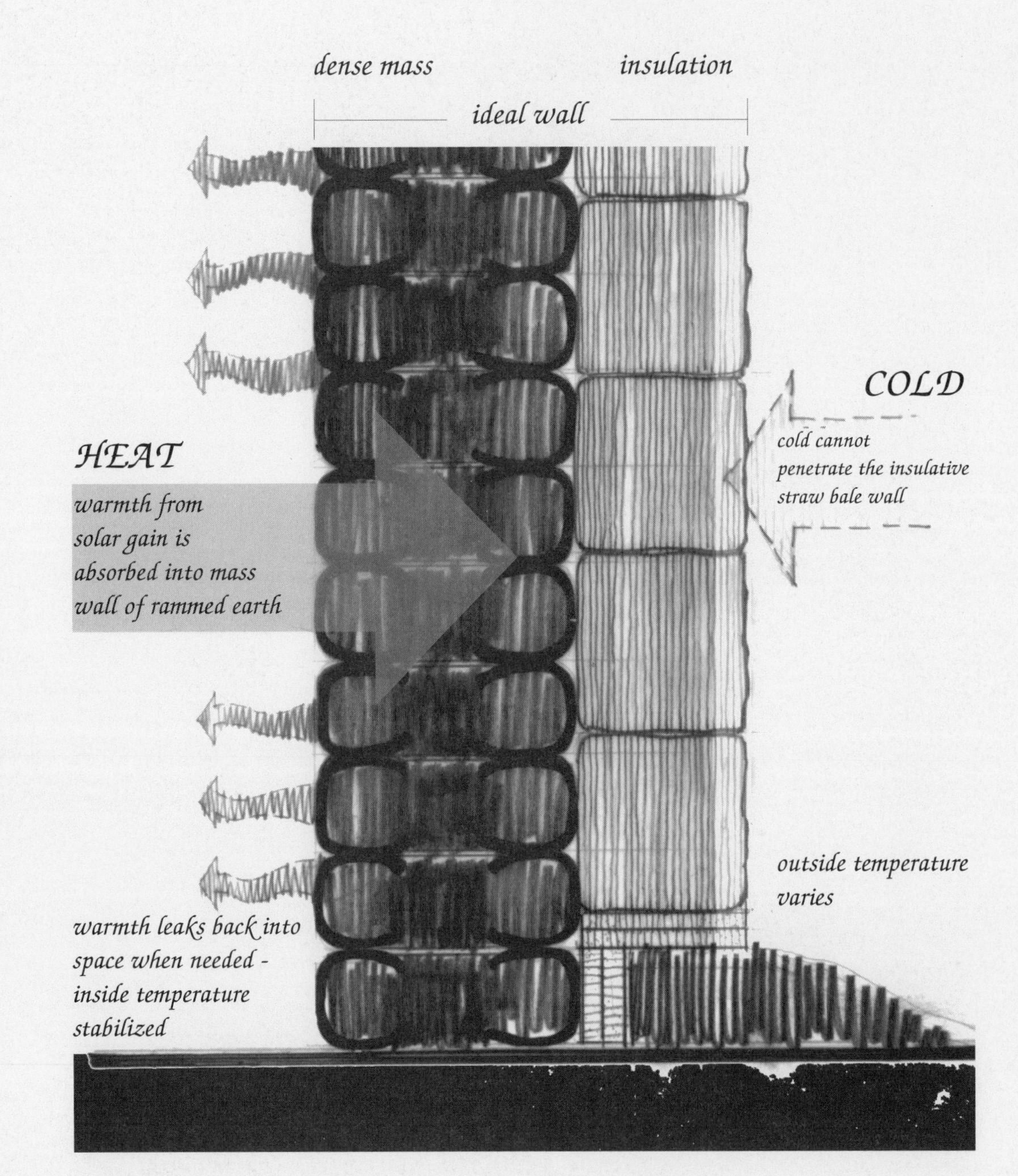

Opposite page - Thermal mass building illustrating the use of the "ideal wall". This building is structured with massive earth rammed tires and insulated on the outside with straw bales.

Experiment

1. Take three glass jars with screw on lids.
2. Leave one empty and fill the other two with water.
3. Put the lids on and put them in the freezer until the water begins to freeze. Don't let them freeze - they will break.
4. Take them all out at the same time and wrap one of the water filled jars with insulation (a couple of wool socks will work).

The air in the empty jar and the water in the other two should all be about the same temperature just as you take them out of the freezer.

No Mass and No Insulation

The jar with only air will warm up very fast to room temperature.

Thermal Mass

The jar with just water (thermal mass) will stay cool much longer as the mass holds the temperature longer than the air. The room temperature will still soon overtake the coolness of the jar.

Thermal Mass and Insulation

The jar that is wrapped with insulation will stay cool the longest as the insulation on the outside of the mass isolates the cool mass from the warmer room temperature.

The experiment will work the same if the jars are put in an oven to warm them up. The empty jar will be the first to cool off. The water filled jar will hold heat longer, and the insulated water filled jar will hold the heat the longest. Use the oven on warm only as a hot oven will break the jars.

The super insulated thermal mass home above works on the same principle. The mass in the building is linked to the tremendous mass of the earth. The heat from the sun is admitted through southern windows and stored in the mass.

Now put a human in a space inside each jar. Let the jars absorb room temperature for an hour and then put them out in the freezing cold winter night. Where is the human going to stay comfortable the longest?

Most shelter, up until recent years, has the human in the empty jar. The temperature outside is the temperature inside unless fuel is continually burned to change the temperature inside. In recent years, due to awareness of the growing shortage of energy, people have applied insulation to help keep the added heat from escaping. This is like an empty jar with insulation around it. Air temperature can be trapped but not stored.

The human in the space surrounded by mass will be warm for a while - until the warmth in the mass leaks out into the surrounding cold air.

The human in the space surrounded by mass and insulation will be the most comfortable for the longest time. The most ideal shelters of the future will make use of this principle.

Thermal mass embodies energy...
Energy establishes comfort in any climate.

South view showing solar glass of thermal mass shelter with insulated mass walls at
the Greater World Community in Taos, New Mexico

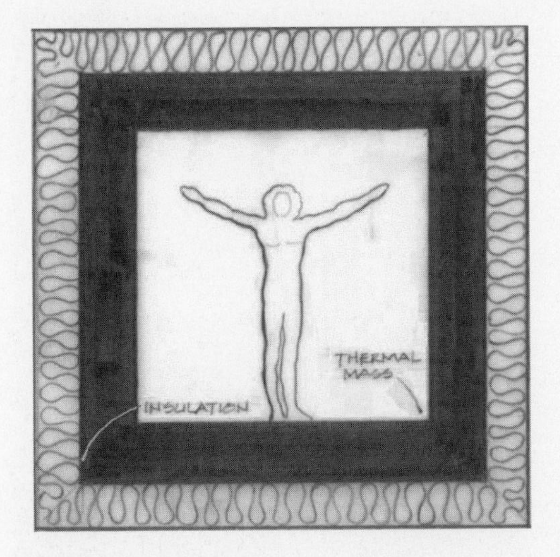

Theoretical Shelter

Effective theoretical shelter of the future would have humans in shelter made of dense mass with insulation around it. The dense mass captures temperature from any source and the insulation keeps it from leaving. This transposes into the schematic shelter diagram above.

Temperature Sources

Knowing how to capture and retain temperature, we look around for the temperature itself.

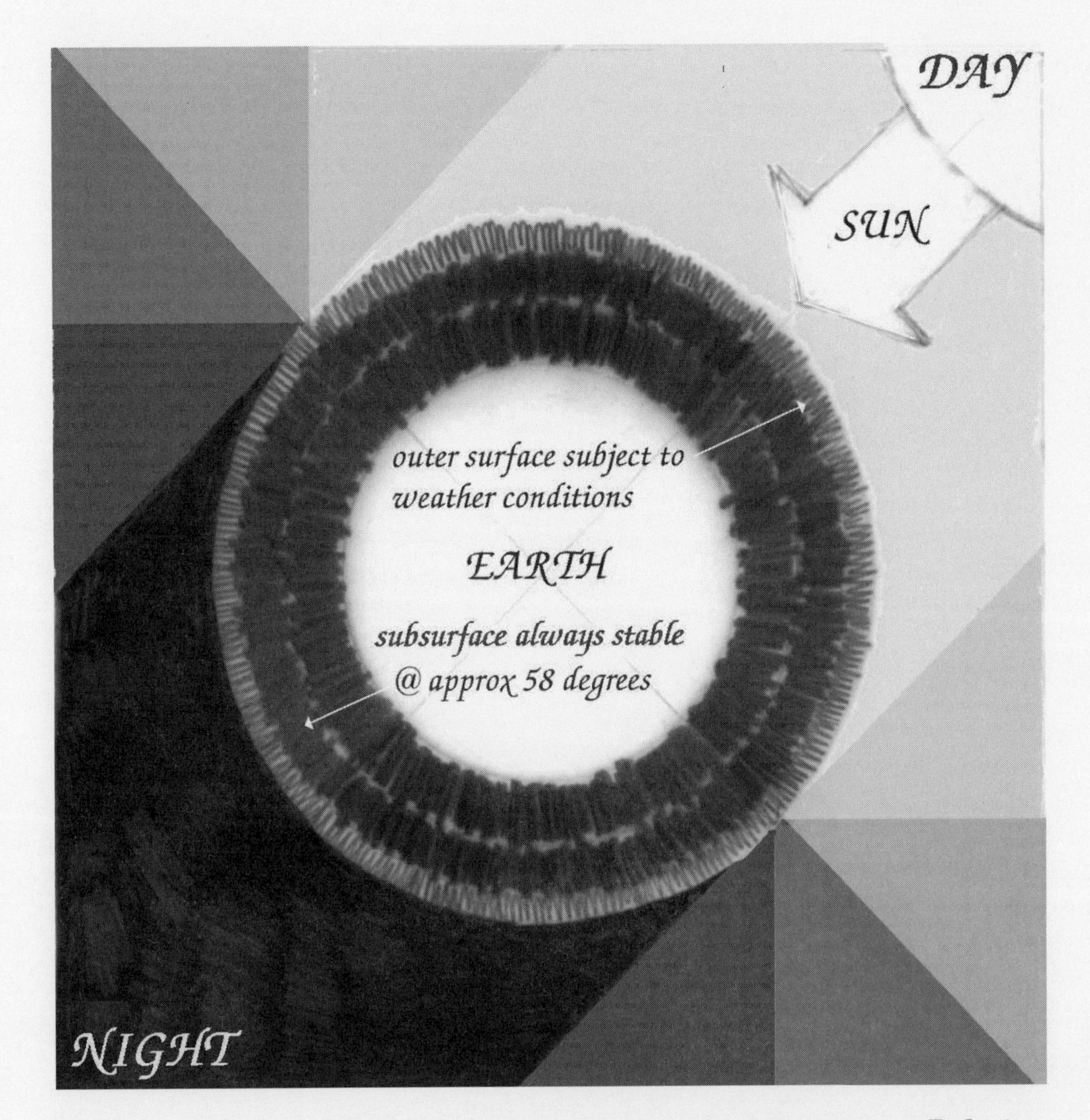

In our world there are two limitless sources of temperature. Relative to temperature of the human body, the subsurface earth is a source of **cool** temperature and the sun is a source of **warm** temperature.

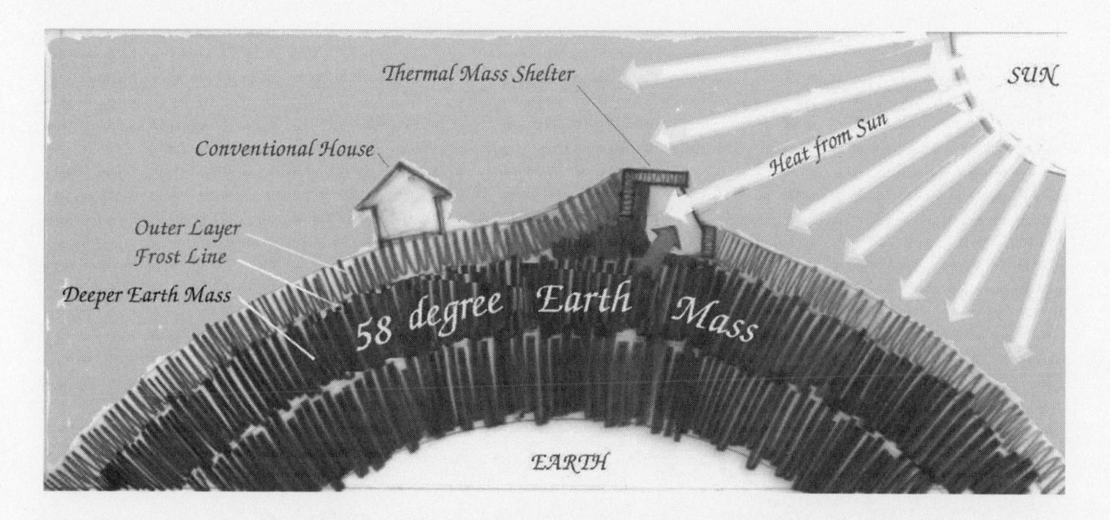

The earth is a thermally stabilizing mass that constantly delivers cool temperature without wires or pipes. The outer few feet of the earth heat up and cool off in response to surface weather. However, deeper in the earth, (about four feet and beyond) the temperature is more constant - around 58 degrees F - and can be used to both cool and stabilize shelter temperature if the shelter is designed to appropriately encounter this phenomenon. The subsurface line, beyond which the earth is a stable temperature, is called the frost line.

The sun is an energy source that delivers heat during the day time without wires or pipes. It can provide a heat source for shelter over much of the planet if the shelter is designed for optimizing solar encounter. In relating a shelter to the sun, it must be observed that the sun is higher in the sky in the summer and lower in the winter due to the tilt of the earth.

Different climates around the globe require different ways of relating the thermal mass shelter to these two sources of temperature - the earth and the sun. Conventional shelter ignores both of these sources of temperature and fails to make use of the free energy therein.

Tuning the Theory

The use of mass to store and subsequently radiate temperature for the comfort of humans is most significantly effective in relation to the height of the human. For this reason mass overhead, which is expensive, is not necessary. Insulation alone is all that is needed overhead. Insulation under the shelter is seldom necessary as it blocks the mass of the shelter from connecting with the mass of the earth which is a major source of cool temperature for stablizing the shelter.

The 58 degrees of the Earth's mass is warm compared to frigid outdoor temperatures of 12 degrees or less. In fact, it is not far from the comfort zone for humans which is considered to be between 70 and 80 degrees. To heat a shelter naturally, admit both the stable Earth mass and the sun. The sun easily heats up the insulated mass of the shelter. The mass stores the heat, and the insulation won't let it escape. The more mass, the more heat it can store. The heat then radiates into the living space from the mass walls when there is no sun. This occurs as heat travels from warmer to cooler areas. If there were no sun for long periods of time, the stable 58 degree mass of the Earth would keep the living space from becoming frigid. Only a small heat source would be needed to bring the temperature up from the stable 58 degrees of the earth to the comfort zone for humans.

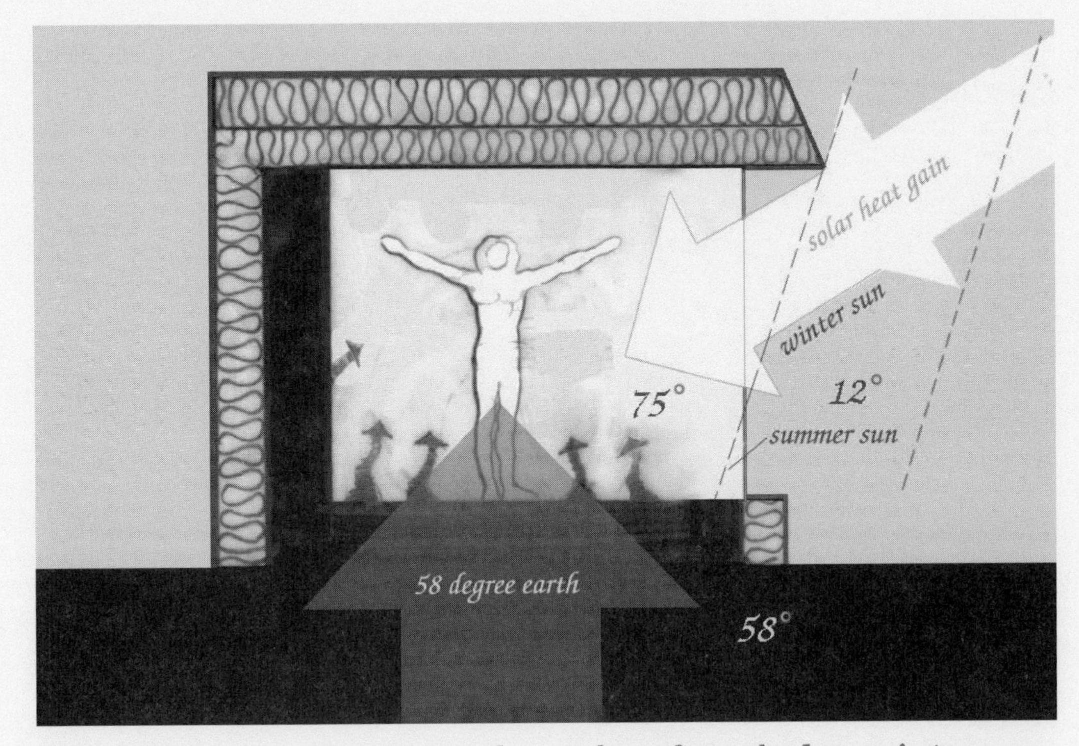

The shelter above can admit and store heat from the **low winter sun**. The heat is stored in the thermal mass walls. The heat is trapped by the outside insulation resulting in a comfortable temperature inside.

This shelter can also block the **higher summer sun** with its overhang and admit cooler earth temperatures by connecting the mass of the shelter directly to the mass of the Earth for summer cooling.

The shelter above is surrounded by thermal mass which is in direct contact with the earth's mass. It is facing north (or away from the sun). The outside temperature is 110 degrees F. The mass of the shelter and the earth, acting as one, pull the temperature of the space down closer to the temperature of the earth mass itself. The result is a stable cooling effect without the use of outside utilities. If the proportion of mass to air volume is tuned correctly, the temperature of the living space can be pulled down to 75 degrees.

Cooling

When it is 110 degrees outside, 58 degrees seems very cool. If you want coolness, you admit the cooler earth temperature and block the sun. The cool mass of the earth is directly connected with the mass of the shelter. The mass of the shelter and earth together pull excess heat out of the living space because heat travels from a warmer to a cooler place.

Connecting the earth's mass to thermal mass strategically built into shelter is like hooking a big battery (the earth) up to a smaller battery (the shelter). The thermal mass of both the earth and the shelter together become an energy storage battery for temperature which makes the living space comfortable in any climate.

Angle of Glass

Heating requires solar exposure. For the most effective solar exposure, the angle of the glass should be perpendicular to the angle of the winter solstice sun. This reduces reflection of the sun and maximizes solar gain in the living space. The winter sun is lower in the sky in the more northern latitudes so **in the far north, vertical glass provides the maximum solar gain**. The southern latitudes, with a higher winter sun, should use sloped glazing to maximimize solar gain. Only high altitudes in these areas get cold enough to require the sloped glass. Other lower altitude, milder areas of southern latitude use vertical glazing. This reduces the intensity of the solar gain thus collecting only moderate heat which is all that is needed.

The glazing angle is thus determined by latitude and altitude.

Right
Interior of sloped glass thermal building

Recessed Buildings

Cooling requires earth exposure. To most effectively cool a shelter, it should be surrounded with earth. The 58 degree deeper earth mass is not far from the temperature of the human comfort zone. Because the surrounding earth mass tends to stablize the temperature in the living space, only a small amount of heat gain is necessary to bring the space up to the comfort zone. The deep earth temperature is more accessible when the building is recessed into the earth. When soil conditions and water tables allow this, it is the preferred approach as it requires less insulation and is a more simple, economical structure than a building on the surface. Where no heating is required, buried buildings are faced away from the sun for no solar gain. This discussion is in reverse for the southern hemisphere.

A thermal building is "tuned" to reach for the sun and/or the Earth as climate requires.

RADIANT HEAT

THERMAL COOL

Surface Buildings

Sites where there is stone or a high water table preventing the recessing of the building into the Earth have the thermal shelter placed on the Earth with insulation all around. **Very cold climates** sometimes require insulation under the floor of a surface building to isolate the thermal mass of the shelter from the cool earth that is subject to frost line temperatures. Sloped glazing (perpendicular to winter sun angle) occurs on the south side to admit maximum warmth of the sun so it can be absorbed by the mass of the shelter. **Warm climates** have no insulation under the floor. This links the mass of the shelter to the cooler mass of the Earth. Vertical glazing occurs on the north side (in the northern hemisphere) leaving the south side solid and blocking solar gain.

WARM CLIMATE

COLD CLIMATE

Right - interior of a surface built thermal mass building in the Greater World Community in Taos, New Mexico

COLD CLIMATE
Day - Night

Warmth travels toward coolness according to the laws of physics. Thermal mass shelter absorbs heat from the sun into the cooler mass during the **day**. At **night** when the air space drops in temperature and becomes cooler than the massive walls, the absorbed heat travels back in to the space. The physics law of thermal dynamics which defines the movement of heat, the periodic solar gain of the sun and the stable mass of the earth provide a heating system that is far more dependable than any fossil fueled system.

For added comfort, insulated shades can be installed on the glass to block heat loss at night. Insulation is doubled on the ceiling where heat loss is greater. Insulation also protects the structure from the earth until it gets below the frost line. Buried or recessed buildings, therefore require less insulation around the envelope of mass.

HOT CLIMATE
Day - Night

During the night, thermal mass shelters lose much heat to the earth through the movement of heat to the cooler earth. This cooling can be enhanced by ventilation which is discussed later. All night the air space is pulled closer and closer to the temperature of the mass of the earth - approximately 58 degrees F. During the day, no solar gain is admitted but heat from the outside air temperature can still come through the glazing. For this reason glazing occurs mostly on the opposite side from the sun and is reduced and/or insulated to prevent as much heat gain as possible. Insulation is again doubled on the roof to prevent heat gain from the sun. The roof should also be a light color to reflect the sun's heat. The strong connection to the mass of the earth is a key factor in pulling the temperature of the living space down to a comfortable level.

Ventilation

Temperature can be controlled in shelter by the interaction between insulated thermal mass and the sun and/or the earth. Fine tuning of this encounter is achieved by ventilation and/or shading. Ventilation is achieved by admitting fresh air low on one end of the space and releasing warmer air at the opposite end through high operable skylights. The natural rising and escape of the warmer air creates a convection current which sucks in the cooler outside air and sweeps it through the space. Shading is executed to simply block incoming sun when necessary.

For more extreme cooling requirements, this incoming air can be taken through tubes recessed deep in the Earth to absorb the Earth's cooler temperature before coming into the shelter. This type of shelter may have no solar gain.

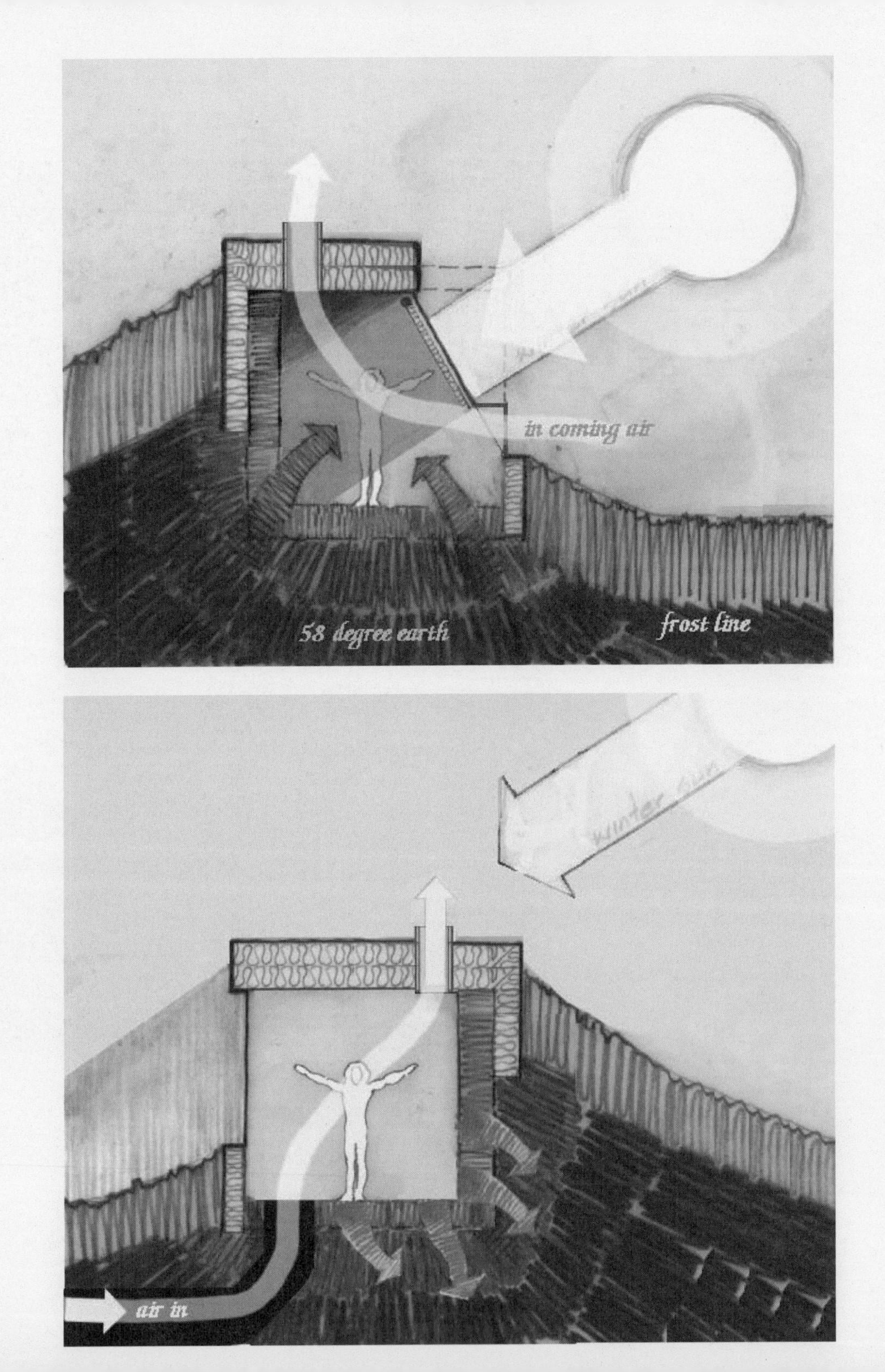

Interior of a ground level thermal mass shelter in Taos, New Mexico

photo credit pg 23 & 27 - Batista Moon

If thermal mass is understood as the stabilizer of temperature, then it must be understood that there is a relationship between the volume of air space to be stabilized and the volume of thermal mass built into the structure. This relationship changes in different climates. Extremely cold or hot climates require more mass relative to the volume of air space in order to give the mass the "edge" over the air volume to be stabilized. This results in smaller spaces with low ceilings in colder climates and small spaces with higher ceilings in hotter climates. More temperate climates can reduce the volume of mass needed resulting in more freedom in the size of living spaces. The fact remains that where serious cooling and/or heating is required, each room must be surrounded in mass and all exterior walls must be insulated below the frost line.

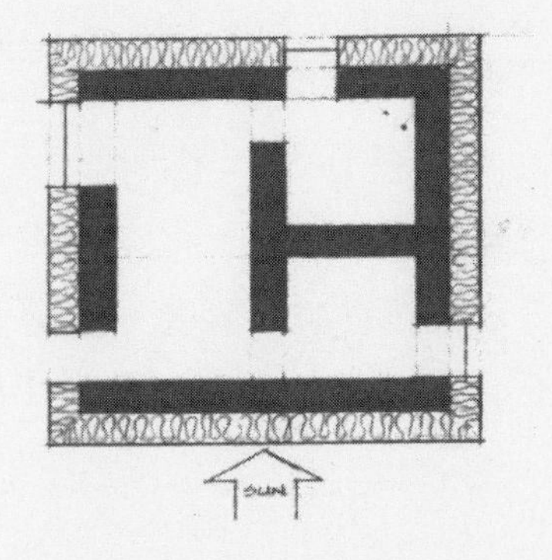

Massive Earthship home in south Texas where cooling is the issue

Cooling with mass requires no solar gain and floor plans can have more conventional layouts.

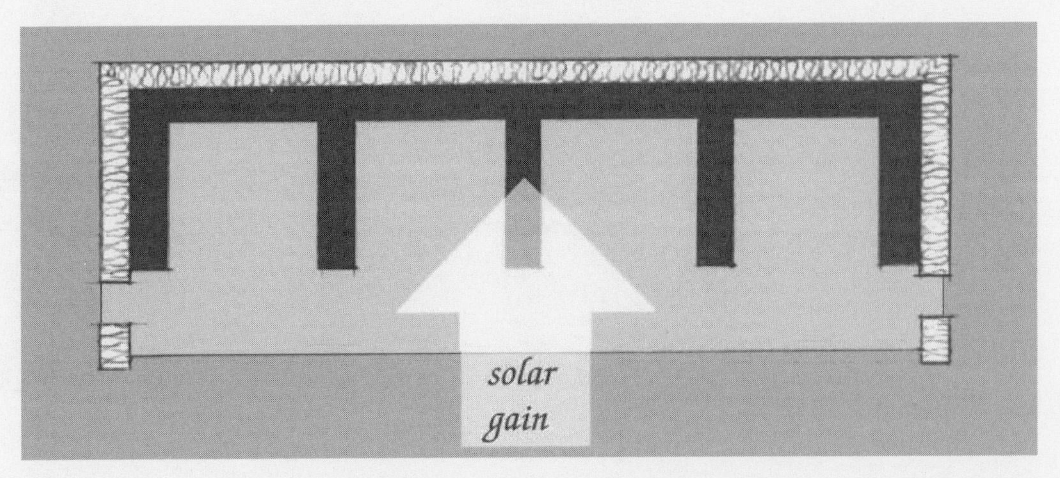

Heating with mass requires admitting solar gain to every space in order to add heat to the mass during the day. This results in linear layouts east to west.

Mass home designed for heat gain in
the Greater World Community in Taos, New Mexico

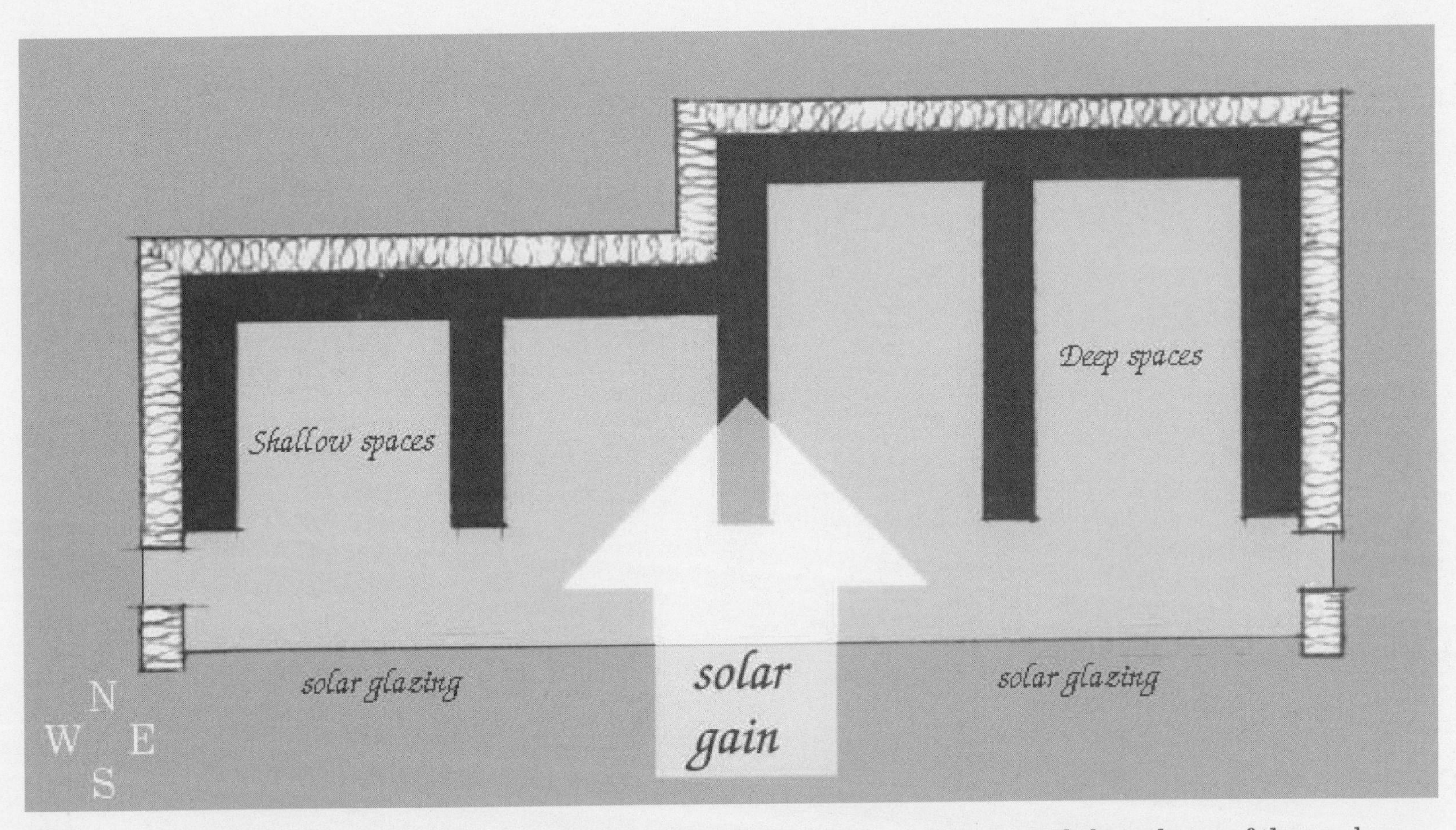

There is an adjustable relationship between the area of solar oriented glazing and the volume of thermal mass surrounding the living space. For a given area of solar glazing, spaces that are deeper in the north/south direction are easier to cool and spaces that are more shallow in the north/south direction are easier to heat. This is put into effect when "tuning" a thermal mass building to its specific climate. In the diagram above, the deeper spaces on the right have the same solar gain as the more shallow spaces on the left. Their depth has increased the amount of air volume to heat as well as the amount of cooling mass available to the space. The result is that they are easier to keep cool. The shallow spaces on the left have less air volume to heat with the same solar gain. Since they are shallow, most of their mass is actually hit by the incoming sun and heated up. The result is that these spaces are easier to keep warm.

If cooling is primary, increase the effect of cooling mass by increasing the north/south depth of rooms and decreasing the east/west width of rooms. This increases the connection to the cooling earth due to the fact that the mass toward the rear of the space will not be hit by the incoming sun leaving it affected only by the cooling earth. Decreasing the east/west width of the space decreases the connection to the warming sun.

If heating is primary, increase the south glazing face and relative solar gain by decreasing north/south depth of rooms and increasing east/west width . This places all mass in a position to be hit by the incoming sun, thus warming the mass and increasing the connection to the warming sun. There is also more solar gain relative to air volume to be heated in this situation resulting in an increased heating potential.

Variations

There are many variations on thermal mass designs relative to latitude, altitude, soil conditions, water tables, etc. Some basic schematic examples follow with conditions opposite in the southern hemisphere.

Extreme Cold, Northern Latitude, Wet Climate

The spaces are small (about 14' x 14') with low ceilings (no higher than 8'). Rooms are lined up facing south. Glazing is vertical because the winter sun is very low in northern latitudes. The vertical glass reduces reflection and loss of solar gain. The building is on the surface of the ground with as much earth pushed up around it as possible. Insulation also occurs under the floor as the surface building cannot permeate the frost line enough to hit the warmer more stable earth mass that is deeper down. A thick massive structure is enveloped in insulation and oriented toward solar gain. The southern vertical glazing has insulated shades to further trap the heat inside at night.

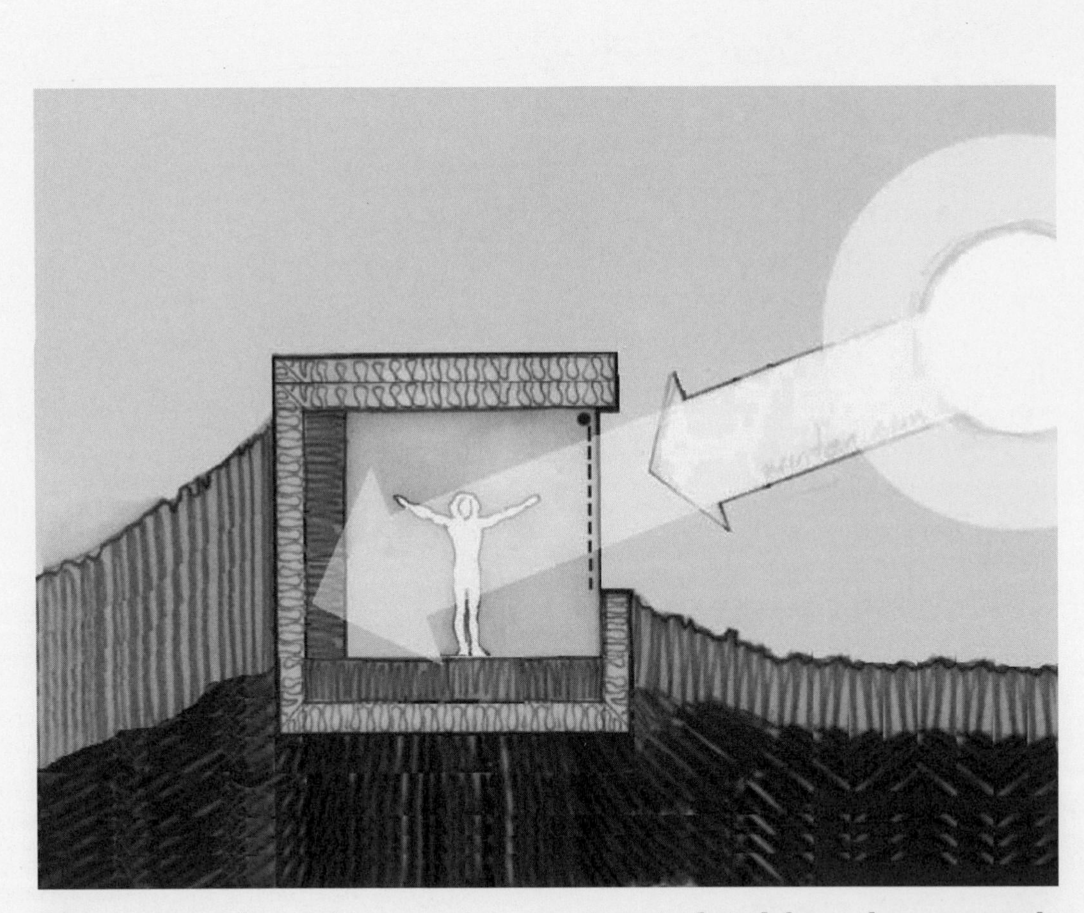

This climate demands a massive structure isolated from the surrounding cold earth by maximum insulation. In this case the mass of the structure is all that can be used for storage of the suns warmth. Southern glass should allow as much solar gain as possible in every room.

Extreme Cold, High Altitude, Southern Latitude, Semi-Arid Climate.

The spaces are small with low ceilings. Rooms are lined up facing south. Glazing is sloped to be perpendicular to the winter sun which is higher than at northern latitudes. This allows maximum solar gain. The building is pushed as deep into the earth as possible and insulated down to the frost line which could be as much as six feet deep. Insulation may not occur under the floor if the building can be pushed deep enough into the earth to fully escape the frost line. The sloped southern glazing may have insulated shades to block heat loss at night. A secondary greenhouse may be added to create a buffer space between the living spaces and the extreme cold outside. This would greatly reduce night time heat loss.

This climate does allow the possibility of earth contact for termal stability if the proper depth is attainable. The stable temperature of the deeper earth, which is enhanced by solar gain, can help warm the living spaces when no sun is avaiable.

Hot and Dry climate, Southern Latitude, Deep Water Table, No Winter, Low Altitude.

The spaces are small with high ceilings. This increases the amount of mass relative to air volume. It also gives the warmer air a place to rise to leaving the potential of maximum cooling in the lower part of the space which is surrounded by cool mass. Glazing is oriented away from the sun resulting in no solar gain to warm the mass. Only the cooling phenomenon occurs. The building is recessed into the Earth as much as possible. No insulation under the floor between earth and living space allows maximum contact with the cool earth. Ventilation comes through underground cooling tubes. These tubes allow the cool earth to take the heat from the air before it enters the building. Operable skylights are larger than standard and shading devices are installed over them. The roof is insulated to the maximum with a light colored finish.

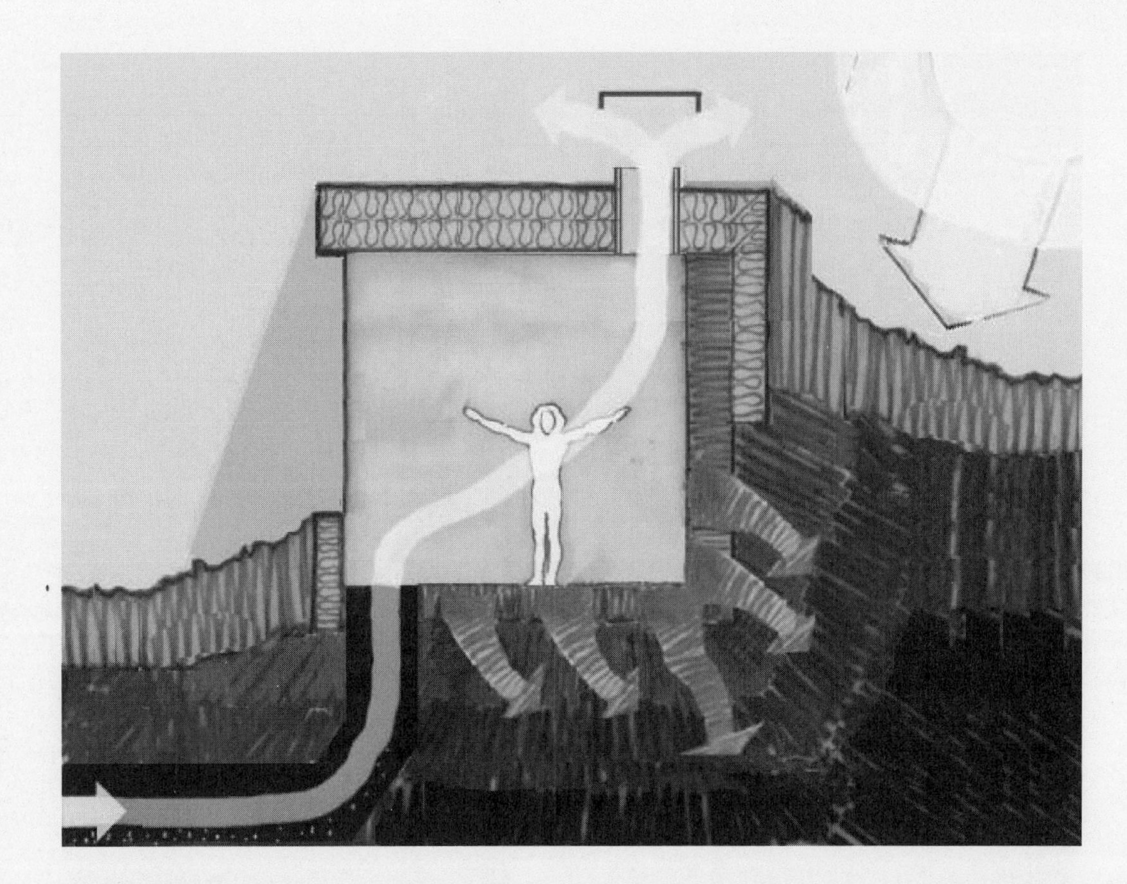

This building has no solar gain and extreme connection to the cooling earth. The mass of the building together with the mass of the earth will pull the temperature of the living space down to a comfortable level.

Hot and Humid Summers, Mild and Wet Winters, Southern Latitude, Low Altitude, High Water Table.

The spaces are medium sized with good ceiling height (up to 10'). The glazing is vertical to minimize solar gain as only a small amount would be needed for the mild winter. An over hang prevents summer sun from entering the space. Some access to solar gain for each room is necessary but the mild winter allows deviation from the lined up rooms all facing south. The building has as much earth bermed up against it as possible to achieve an adequate volume of thermal mass. No insulation occurs under the floor as a connection to the cool earth is needed. Ventilation comes through underground cooling tubes to cool the incoming air. The moisture in the hot incoming air tends to condense on the sides of the tube that are against the cool earth. This results in a natural dehumidifying effect before the air enters the space.

This building is on a compacted pad built up off of the existing grade because of the high water table. The earth mass is separated from the building mass by plastic vapor barriers. A plastic vapor skirt also surrounds the building to direct surface moisture from the building. Only cement based plasters are used in this climate. The spaces are deeper in the north/south direction to increase the ratio of mass to solar gain.

Hot and Dry Summers, Mild Winters, Southern Latitude, Moderate Altitude, Deep Water Table.

The building is buried as completely as possible for connecting with the cool earth. There is no insulation between the building and the earth. The spaces are medium sized and can have higher ceiling heights if desired. The glazing is vertical to minimize solar gain as only a small amount would be needed for the mild winter. An over hang prevents summer sun from entering the space. Some access to solar gain for each room is necessary but the mild winter allows deviation from maximum solar gain for each room.

Ventilation is taken through under ground cooling tubes and naturally convected out the high operable skylites. In extreme heat cases, the skylight is solar enhanced to facilitate better convection.

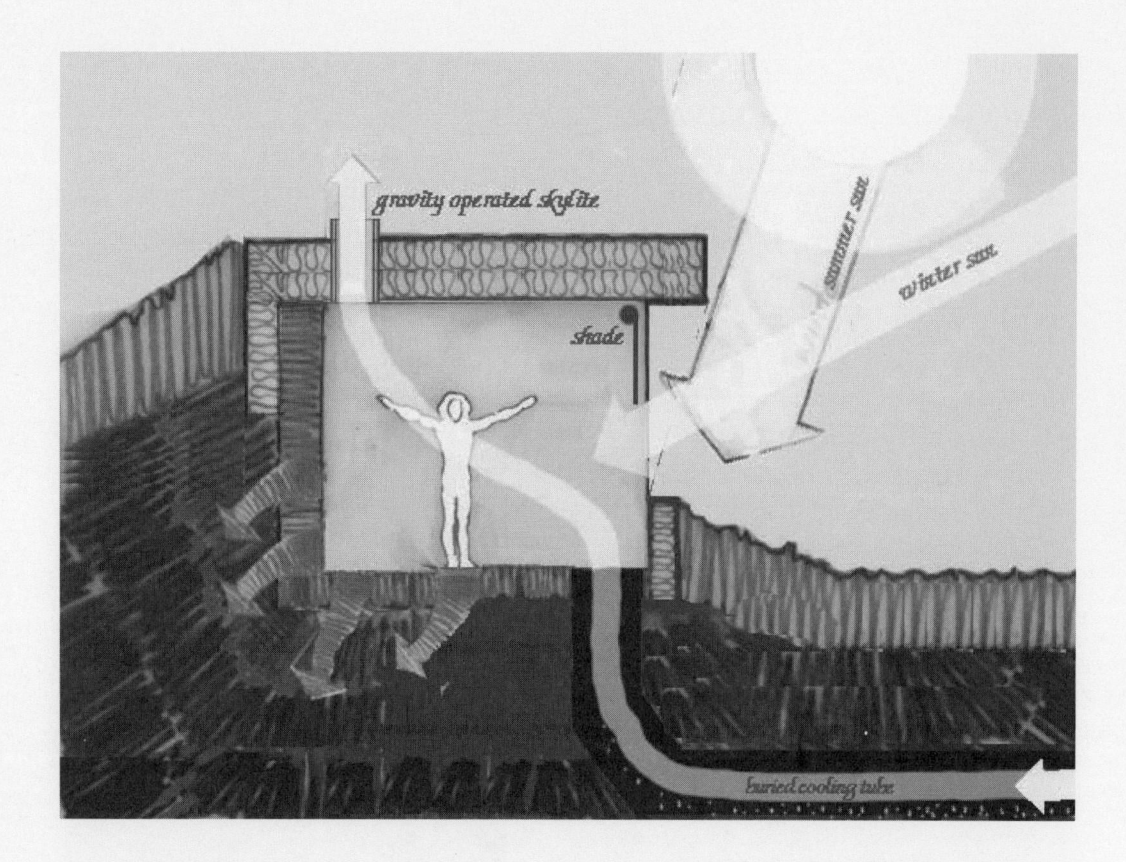

This building has a very strong connection to the cool earth with perimeter insulation only occuring as protection from surface temperatures. Roof insulation is maximum (R 80) and the roof is a light color to reflect the hot summer sun.

Insulated shades on the glass face block unwanted spring and autumn sun as well as insulate away from extreme summer heat.

Prevailing Cloudy Skies, Cold and Damp Winters, Warm and Wet Summers, Northern Latitude, Low Altitude, High Water Table.

The building would not be recessed in the earth because of the high water table. Earth would be built up around the building as much as possible to create burial mass. Plastic vapor barriers would wrap a raised building pad. a plastic skirt would surround the building just below finish burial.

Perimeter insulation would isolate the interior mass from the damp cold earth down to about five feet below burial. Here the earth temperature is stable at approximately 58 degrees F. Vertical glass on the south side of the building would maximize very low winter sun. Higher winter sun would still be welcome in the space to store warmth for cooler, cloudy days.

This building would be built of mass that is isolated from the surface dampness but connected to the more stable deeper earth temperature. The isolated mass of the structure as well as the deeper earth mass under the floor would be warmed by admitting every ray of sun that shines in between the cloudy days. When no sun is shinning on winter days, the slightly warmed, deeper earth temperature would stabilize the space requiring minimal back up heating. Very little cooling would be necessary in the summer and this would easily be handled by the operable roof skylite.

Clearstory

The addmition of sun through high windows over another space is often used to get solar gain to a space deep in the northern side of a building. This solar gain is aimed at mass walls on the rear (north side) of the space. There are some situations where this is necessary and it does add light and some solar heat gain. There are, however, a few down side realities to this approach. It creates a very high ceiling which is where the heat will go. In that the highest place in the room is where the glass is, the heat loss out the glass in this approach is significant. This results in almost as much loss as gain. This approach also creates more complicated structure and detailing resulting in more expense. For these reasons, this approach should only be used when the downsides are understood and not where economy and high performance are serious concerns.

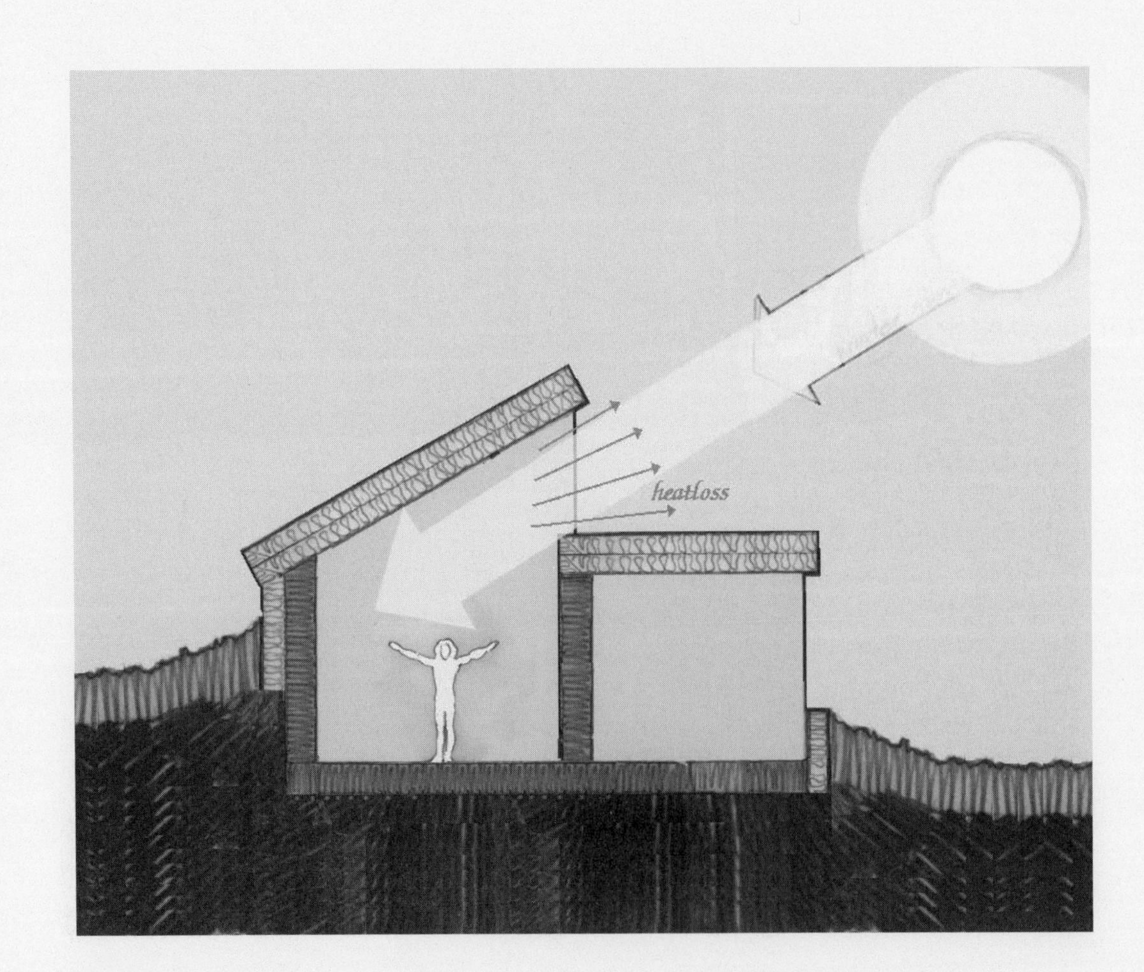

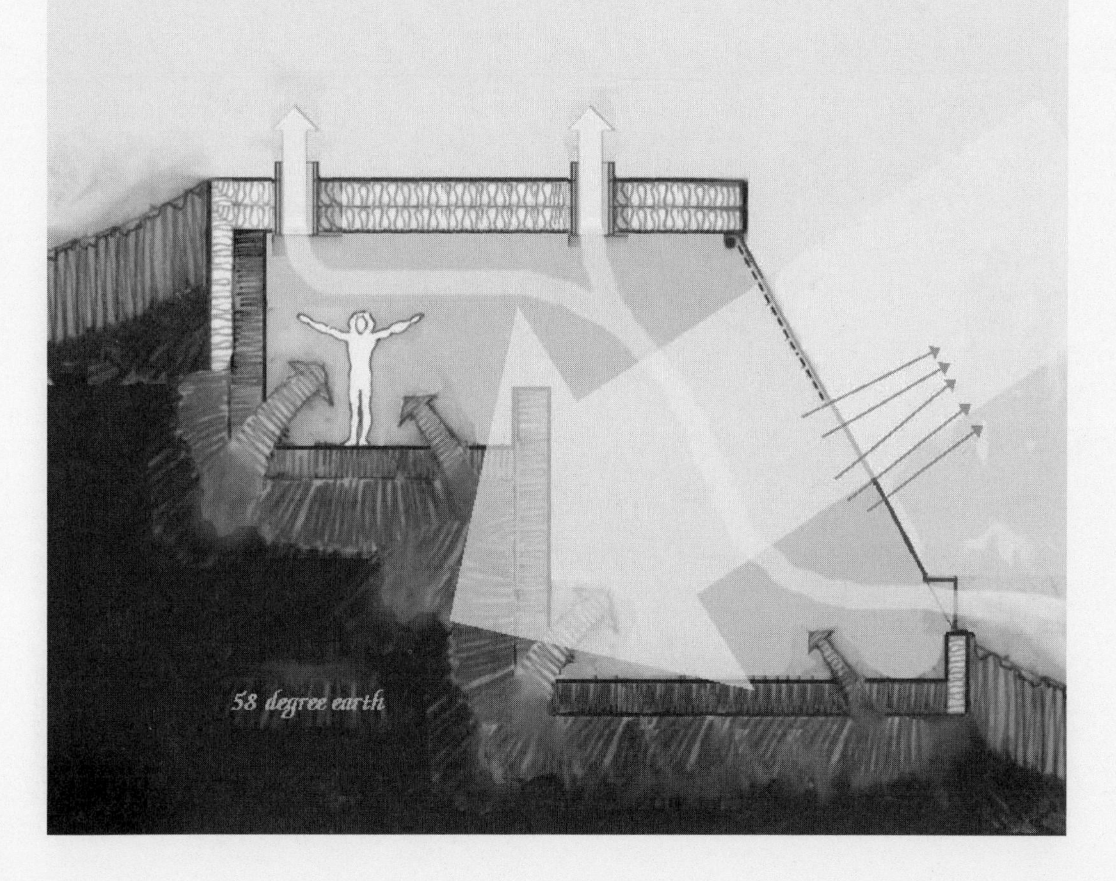

Two Story

The use of two story spaces creates a dynamic spacial experience and is good for growing large plants and trees. It also presents significant heat loss and the need for solar control (shading) in most cases. The two story space will be cooler in the coldest part of the winter and tend to over heat without shading in the summer. Operable insulated shading helps control both of these effects but, again, this method should be used only with an understanding that performance and cost will be affected.

Upper rooms over looking two story spaces tend to be warmer than the two story space and their use should be designated accordingly. Natural convection ventilation is enhanced by the height in these taller spaces. The ventilation can be designed to include or bypass the overlooking spaces.

The Shape of the Future

If any shelter anywhere on the planet incorporates both mass and insulation and admits an appropriatly regulated amount of both the sun and the earth temperatures, it will not need manufactured and delivered energy for heating and cooling purposes. Thermal mass and solar gain must therefore be a factor of shelter in living vessels of the future. Buildings, communities and cities will reflect this physical encounter with planetary phenomena. Humanity and the earth will be free from the "price" of conventional temperature control and there will be comfort in any climate.

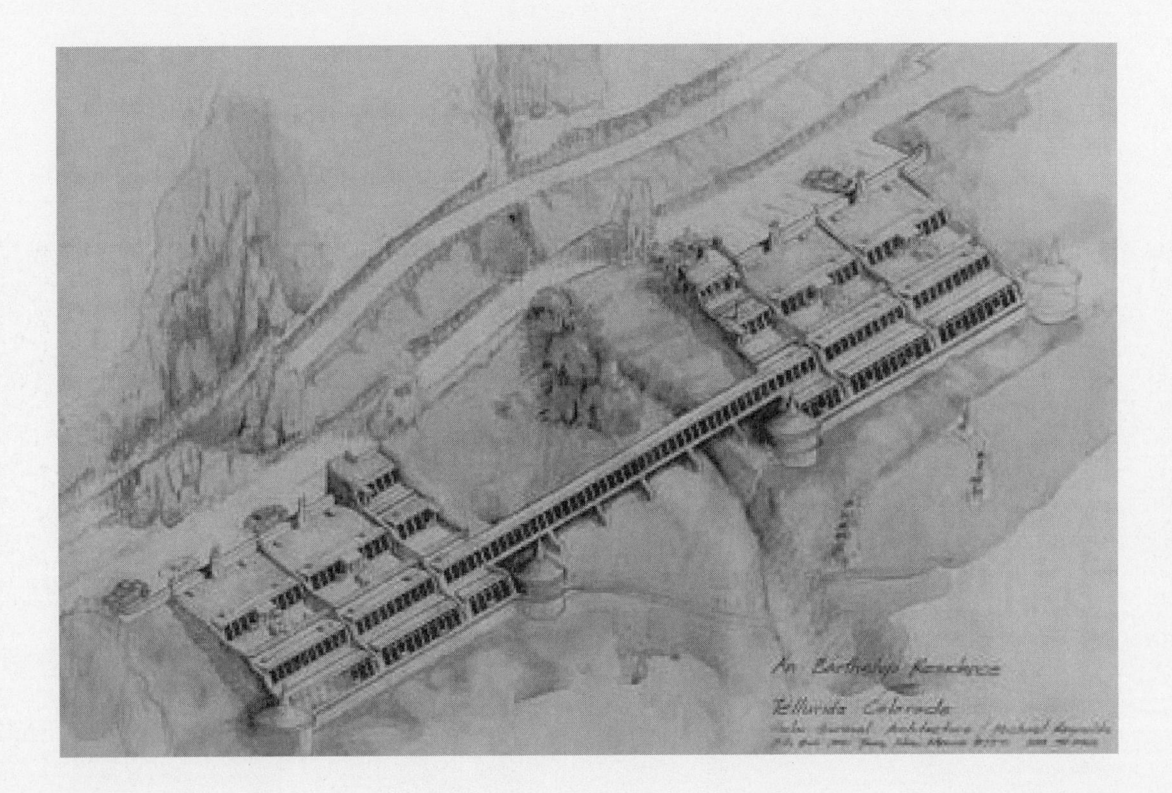

From condos, to colonies, to cities, the future could present a different and softer interaction between people and planet.

Application

comfort in any climate

There are many ways of building thermal mass into a structure. Rock, concrete, rammed earth and adobe are all effective. When choosing a globally universal method of providing both thermal mass and structural integrity in a single component, one must consider cost, global availability, environmental issues, structure, population vs. resources and user- friendliness. After twenty-five years of research in this realm, used automobile tire casings rammed with earth to create dense massive round structural bricks have proven to be one of the most appropriate ways to achieve structural mass in shelter. Scrap tires are as plentiful as trees all over the planet, and more tires are constantly being discarded. They provide a perfect "low tech" form for earth-rammed bricks. This results in a very substantial and versatile mass building technique.

The landscape of the United States is cluttered with an estimated 2 billion scrap tires. Of the 253 million scrap tires generated each year, 46% end up stockpiled in landfills according to the Scrap Tire Management Council. Used tires are a natural resource material indigenous to the entire planet. They are available for more productive use than discarding them in landfills.

"The benefits of using scrap tires are particularly enhanced if they can be used to replace virgin construction materilas made from nonrenewable resources." 1

1 Engineering Properties of Tire chips and soil Mixtures. Environmental Geotechnics report No. 95-2. Edil, T. B. and Bosscher, P. J.., 1993; department of civil and Environmental engineering, University of Wisconsin; Madison, Wisconsin.

Earthships

An Earthship is an autonomous thermal mass dwelling unit that has been evolving in New Mexico for thirty years. The major building component of the Earthship is used automobile tires filled with compacted earth to form a rammed earth brick encased in steel belted rubber. These bricks and the resulting bearing walls they form are virtually indestructible. The three foot thick massive walls and the method of incorporating them into the earth create living spaces that maintain a constant temperature. Thus, with natural ventilation systems built in, an Earthship home will heat itself in the winter and cool itself in the summer without the use of centralized fossil or nuclear fuels.

Small Earthships may use as few as 200 scrap tires while larger structures, such as actor Dennis Weaver's "Earth Yacht", may use as many as 7000 scrap tires in their construction.

Rationale

The rubber automobile tire rammed with earth provides an appropriate building block for a vessel that aligns with the environmental phenomena of the planet. The rubber automobile tire is indigenous all over the world as a "natural resource". It can be harvested with absolutely no technical devices or energy other than two human hands to pick it up and throw it into a pickup truck. Tires can be used as found without any modification. The rubber tire casings provide an ideal form for manageable production of thermal mass building blocks with little more than human energy. Pounding tires full of earth requires low specific skills. People of all shapes and sizes can be taught to pound a tire. The skill requires physical energy more than brute strength.

"You don't pound tires with your head, you pound with your body and your body learns the intensity of thermal mass"

k. jacobsen

Pounding earth into tire casings to make thermal bricks above - tire work on an earthship

Structure

The structural concept of the Earthship is based on various curvilinear shaped room modules for thermal and structural purposes. The modules usually accomodate both mass and structure and admit sun on the south as required. Operable skylights for ventilation are placed in the ceiling above the mass room module. Earth may be bermed around the mass walls to provide more mass. The structure, mostly earth itself, is based on the concept of very wide walls and even distribution of loads. The 2'-8" wide massive walls of the Earthship are wide enough to surpass conventional requirements for structural load distribution to the earth. Earthship walls are thus wider than the required footing for such a wall. The massive, load bearing walls of the Earthship are structural monoliths which are their own foundations while also providing temperature stabilization for the spaces they enclose.

Code Acceptance

Earth-rammed tires have been a code accepted building method for twenty years. Building permits for Earthships have been granted in many counties across the United States. Earthships exist in Bolivia, Australia, Mexico, Japan, Canada, South Africa, Russia, Belgium and all over the United States. Based on a series of tests on tire constructed walls at the home of Dennis Weaver in Ridgeway, CO, engineer Tom Griepentrog, P.E. has stated, "It is my opinion that the construction method is equivalent to or better than the general quality, strength, effectiveness, fire resistance, durability and safety that is required by the Uniform Building Code."

The tire walls are strong and resilient. "Based on observations and reported tests, it would appear that the tire walls are not as brittle as an adobe or rammed earth wall of comparable thickness. This means that the wall can deform further than an adobe wall without losing strength....Lateral force tests were conducted which indicate a high coefficient of friction between the running bond of tires, as would be expected. The presence of the tires should allow much more in-plane and out-of-plan deformation in the walls than in an equivalent adobe wall without the formation of large diagonal cracks." An extensive engineering evaluation for earth-filled tire construction is available from Solar Survival Press.

EVALUATION OF THE SEISMIC PERFORMANCE
OF ALTERNATIVE CONSTRUCTION MATERIALS IN NEW MEXICO

Prepared for the Federal Emergency Management Agency
by
Wiss, Janney, Elstner Associates, Inc.
under the
National Earthquake Technical Assistance Contract
EMW -92-C-3852, task Assigment 63
WJE No. 952009
May 7, 1995

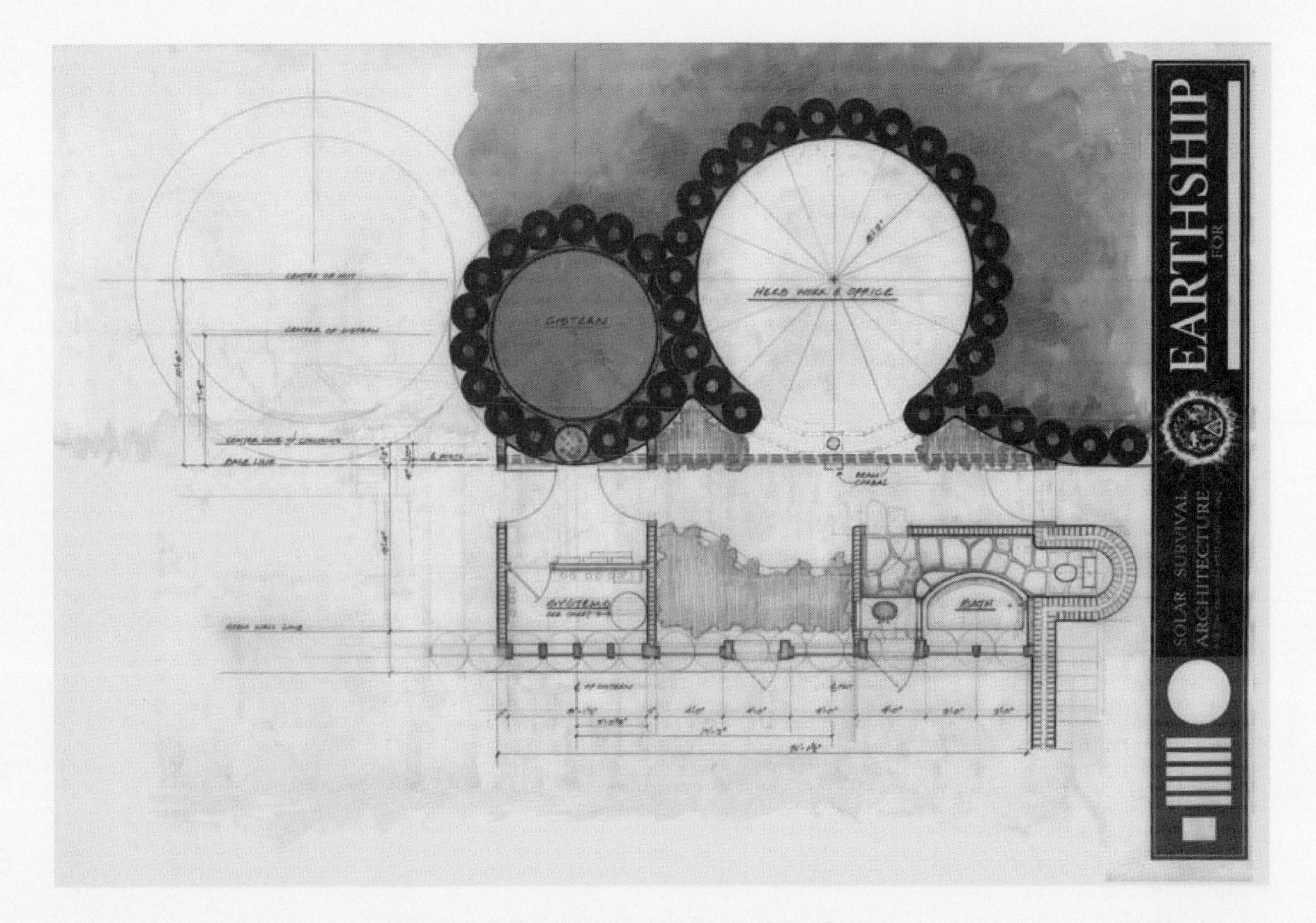

Floor plan of a Hut Earthship in Belgium with circular rooms

Method

Tire walls are made by laying tires in staggered courses like brick or concrete block. Each tire is filled with compacted earth, so that it becomes a rammed earth brick. A pounded tire weighs over 300 pounds, therefore, all tires are pounded in place and only minor movements can be made after the tire is fully pounded.

The tires are set on leveled undisturbed ground and pounded in place using a sledge hammer. Each tire takes about three or four wheelbarrows of dirt. The tires are pounded level in all directions. Scrap cardboard is used to fill in the holes in the tires and make the them temporarily contain the earth on all courses other than the first course which is flat on the ground. Since both sides of the tire wall will eventually be buried or covered by plaster, the cardboard could decompose without affecting the structure.

When the tire module has been constructed, two continuous wood collar plates are anchored to the top course of the tire walls with 3' long rebar stakes (see diagram on following page). This serves as a bond beam or "tie plate" and also receives the trusses for the roof structure. This bond beam is also sometimes built with concrete. A greenhouse for solar gain is framed-up on the sun side of the curvilinear massive spaces. The roof of this thermal mass building should have a minimum of R-60 to ensure minimal heat loss. Once the roof and greenhouse are installed, the voids between the tires on the inside are packed out with mud or concrete. Cans and bottles or rocks are used as spacers to reduce the amount of mud or concrete needed. Packing out the tire wall creates a smooth surface for the final plaster coat. Clean roofing techniques that leach nothing into the water are used to provide catchwater for household use. Moisture barriers of 6 mil plastic are added as a "skirt" around the building to isolate the mass from surface water.

Placing tire

Placing cardboard

Earthrammed tire

Pack out

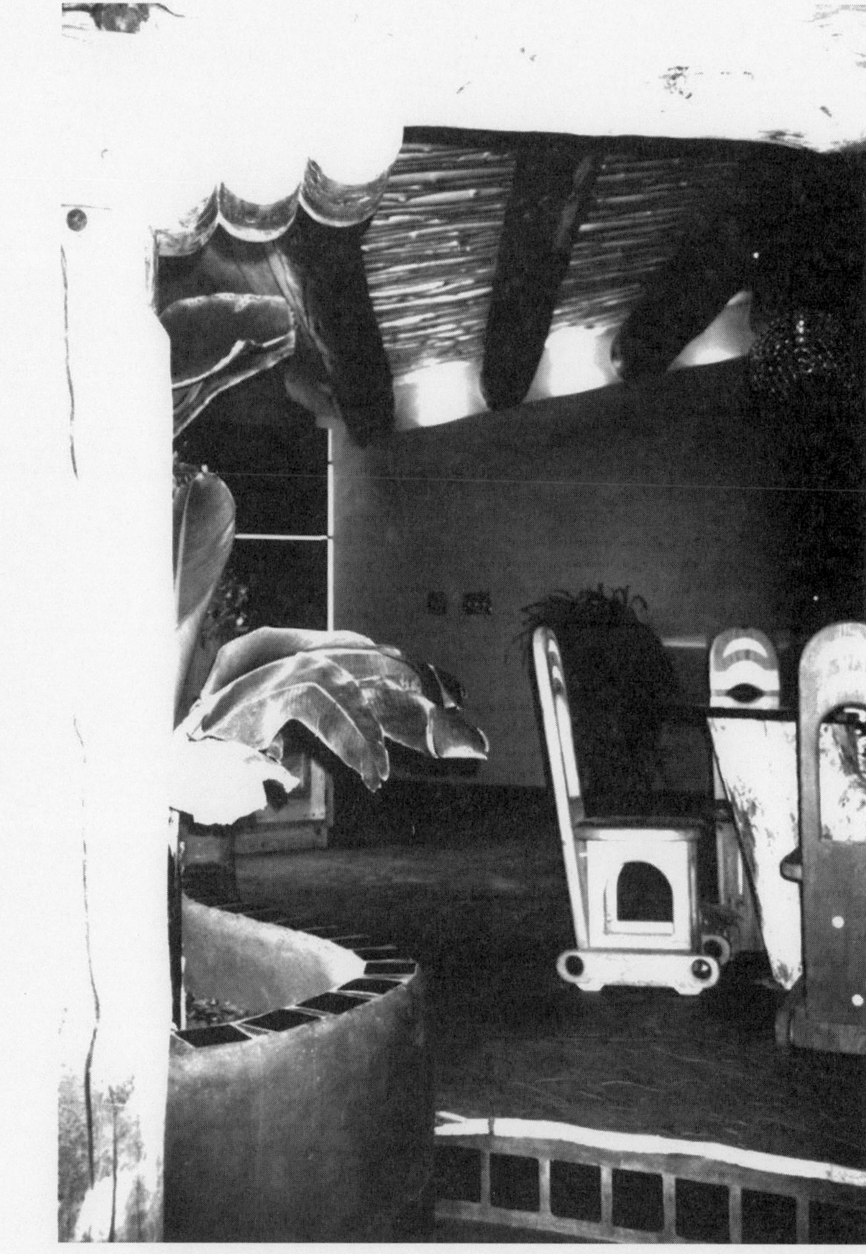

Finish plastered tire wall

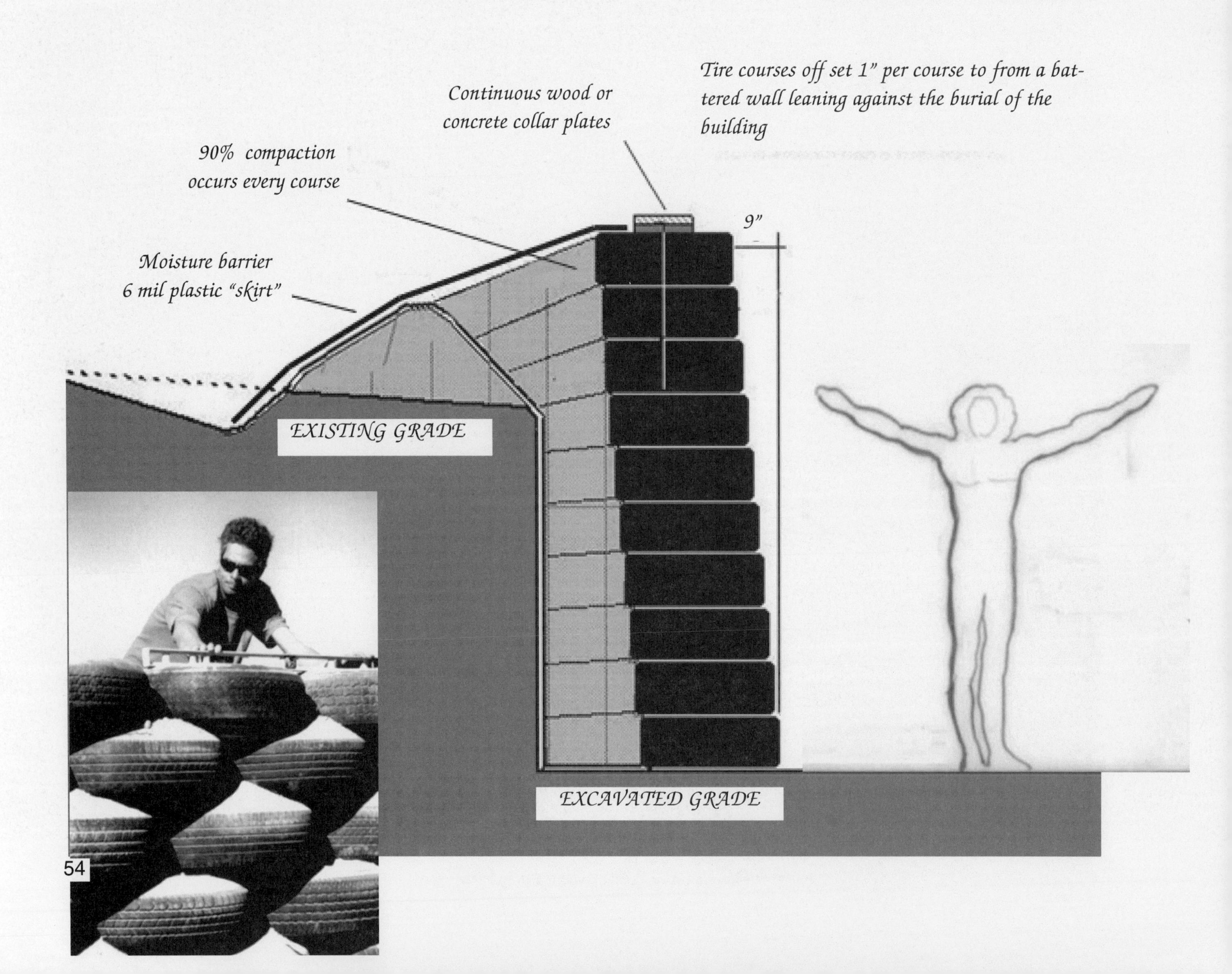
Tire courses off set 1” per course to from a battered wall leaning against the burial of the building
Continuous wood or concrete collar plates
90% compaction occurs every course
Moisture barrier 6 mil plastic “skirt”
9”
EXISTING GRADE
EXCAVATED GRADE

Battered earth rammed tire wall leaning in to burial

Above Ground Earthship

Any passive solar building needs both insulation and thermal mass. Standard Earthships have circumvented the need for wall insulation because the earth rammed tire walls are recessed into the earth. Earthships that are not buried require insulating the outside of the tire walls. Straw bale veneer is the most economical insulator with regards to price, time and R-factor in this case.

Design Variations

The basic U module and the circle Hut module are the most efficient room structures for earth rammed tire construction. These rooms are usually linked with a greenhouse hallway where heating is an issue. However, other designs have been built. Because of the extreme heat and humidity in Texas, a tire hacienda was designed and built with no direct solar gain (see page 30). The tire walls were built without curves. The straight, tall tire walls were reinforced with concrete or tire buttresses and columns. Because of their massive nature, rammed earth tire walls should not exceed ten feet in height without a concrete bond beam.

The vertical faced Earthship shown under construction at right is one of the most economical units available. It can be any size from an efficiency unit up to four bedrooms and two baths.

For more information on Earthship options, designs, construction drawings and consultation, contact...

Earthship Biotecture
PO Box 1041
Taos, New Mexico
87571

www.earthship.org
biotecture@earthship.org
earthshipbiotecture.com
ph 505 751 0462
fax 505 751 1005

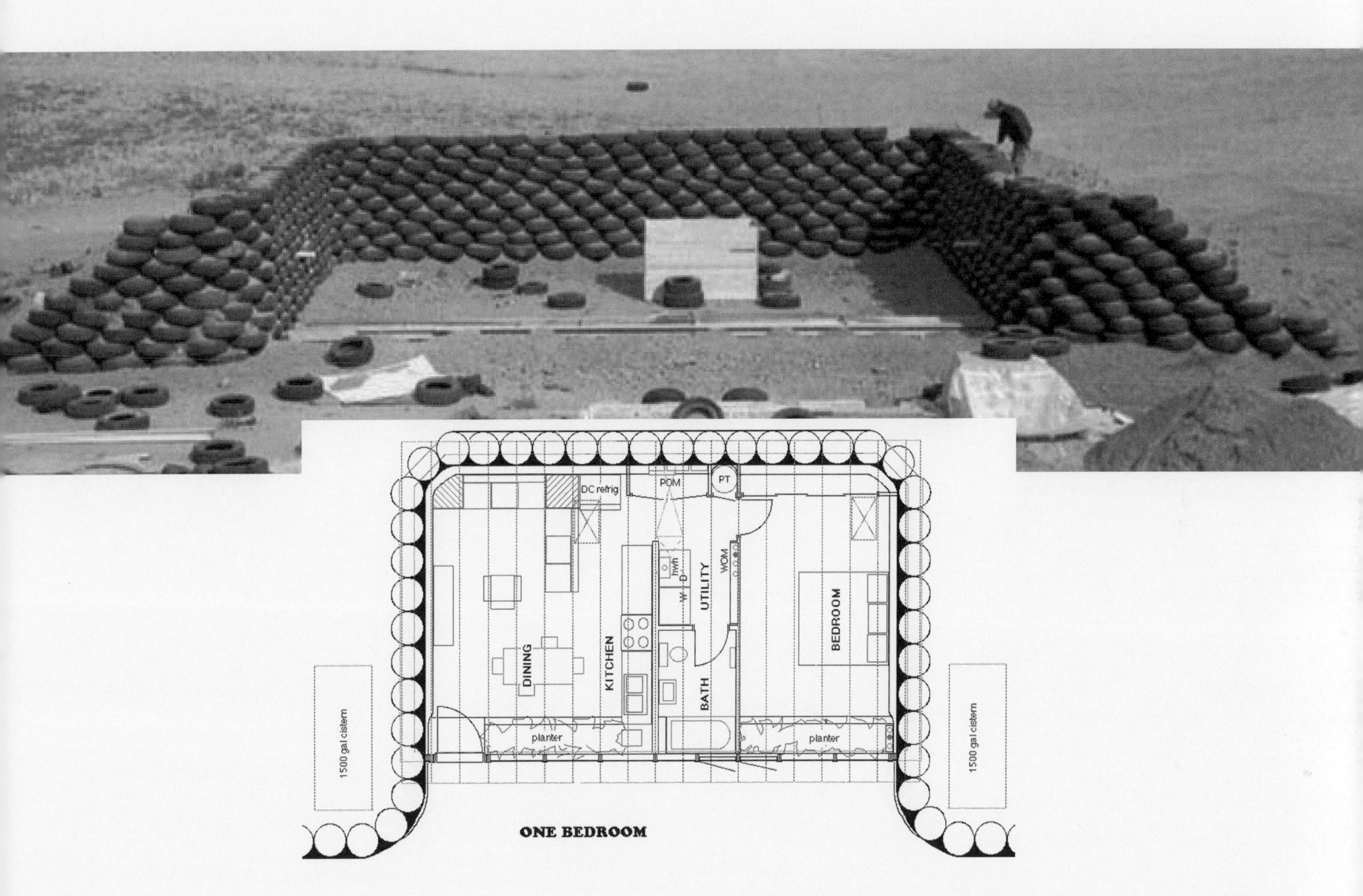
DC refrig
POM
PT
hwh
W
D
UTILITY
WOM
BEDROOM
DINING
KITCHEN
BATH
planter
planter
1500 gal cistern
1500 gal cistern

ONE BEDROOM

The Quality of the Space

There is an extensive study by the University of Wisconsin-Madison regarding the use of scrap tires in civil and environmental construction. Within the study, the authors state "recent research indicated that shredded tires do not show any likelihood of being a hazardous waste material or of having adverse effects on ground water quality."

Tires used in Earthships are buried behind 1.5 to 6 inches of plaster and esentially sealed from the living space. Exposure to conventional carpet can be more hazardous than plaster covered tires. Perhaps more telling is the fact that hundreds of people have lived in tire buildings over the past 25 years with no reported complaints about the quality of life. In fact the reports are to the contrary. People love the "feeling" of these massive earthen homes.

Fire

Similar to the concern regarding quality of space is the concern of fire. People think that because tire piles in tire dumps burn so easily and are so hard to put out, that an earth-rammed tire wall would act similarly. Compare a pile of tires with air all around to a lightly crumpled newspaper. Both torch easily due to adequate air circulation around flammable materials. Compare an earth-rammed tire wall that is plastered with mud or cement both sides to a New York City phone book. Both are very difficult to catch fire and keep burning because of the density of the materials and lack of air circulation.

One of the many devastating forest fires that hit New Mexico in the summer of 1996 was the Hondo fire, which devoured many conventional homes. An Earthship was caught in the middle of the fire. The roof, front face, and all the wood on the inside were burned away. The only parts of the building that were not destroyed were the earth-rammed tire walls and the aluminum can/cement walls. The structure of the building was left usable, and a new roof and front face are planned to be installed.

Conclusion

There are many ways to achieve thermal mass in the structure of a dwelling. There are good arguments for many materials. **The more important issue is that thermal mass be built into all shelters of the future regardless of what material is used to create the mass.**

Earthship burned out in a forest fire in New Mexico
- tire walls still standing - all else gone

A Rock and a Feather

A rock and a feather are released from a high cliff. The rock plummets to the ground while the feather meanders around in the air. The feather is so light that it takes on some of the characteristics (currents) of the air it is falling through. Consequently the journey of the feather is indefinitely long while the journey of the rock is very short.

Humans and trees are are placed on the earth. Humans plummet into jeapordy in a few thousand years while trees stay around for millions of years. The trees are interfaced with the earth as they encounter the characteristics of the environment they are living in. Because of this the journey of trees is indefinitely long. The journey of humanity, however may be very short unless we can learn from the tree.

Every aspect of a tree is generally a contribution to its environment. Trees are constantly supporting an environment that supports trees. This is why trees have been around for so long.

Most aspects of humanity are a detriment to their environment. Humans are constantly detroying an environment that supports humans. This is why humanity may not be around indefinitely.

Encounter, adaptation and contribution
are the fuels that will take humanity into the future.

Detail of the Shell House in Taos, New Mexico

above - a rose grown inside an Earthship in the winter
below - Earthship condo design for Telluride, Colorado

Earthship at 9,500 feet elevation in northern New Mexico

Below and right - views of a sloped faced thermal mass structure in the Greater World Community in Taos, New Mexico
Left - detail of the same building

photo credits left to right - Alix Woosley, Kirsten Jacobson, Jonah Reynolds

Above and right - circular “Hut” type Earthship drawings for a thermal mass building in Belgium

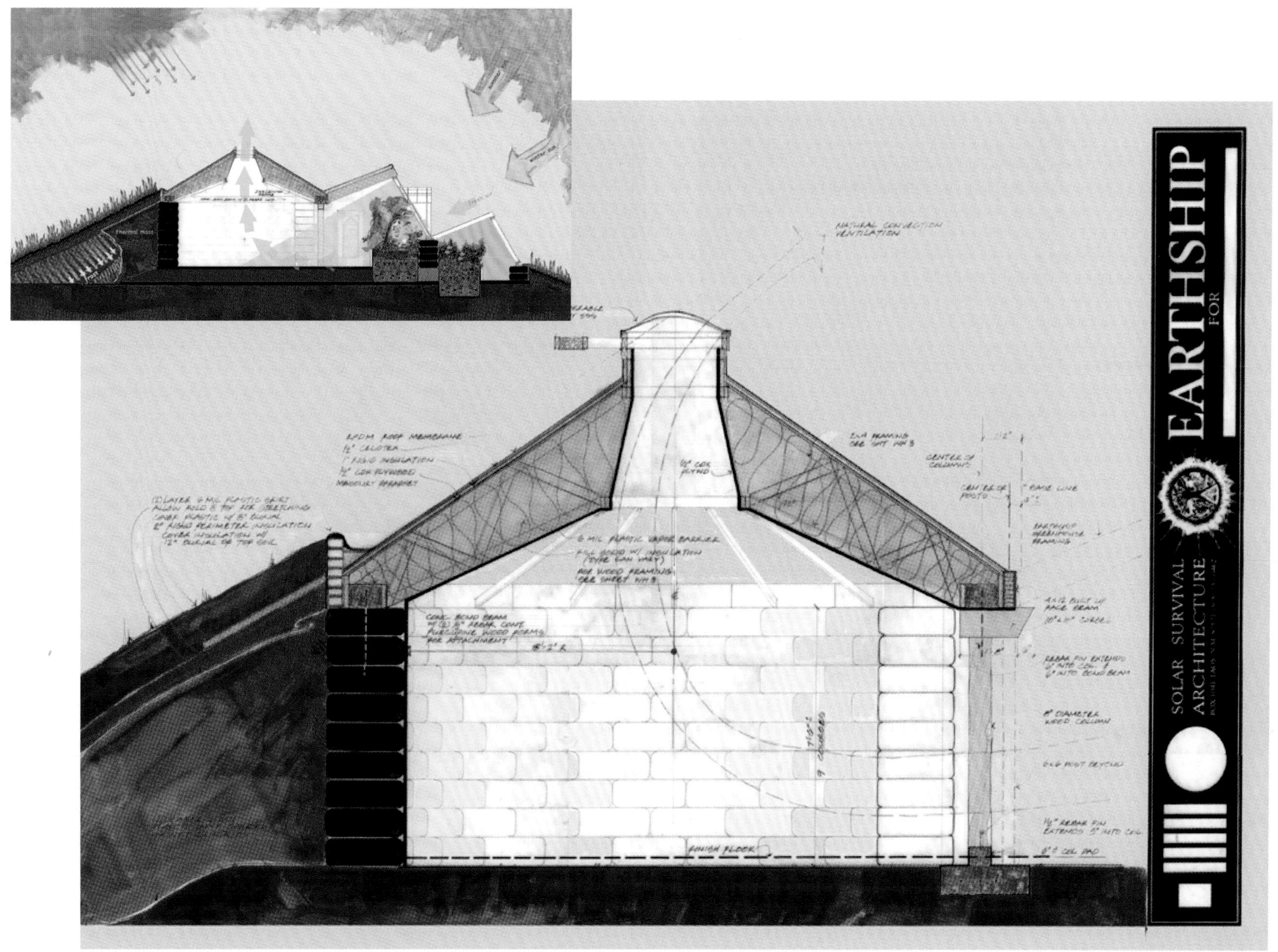
EARTHSHIP
FOR
SOLAR SURVIVAL
ARCHITECTURE
NATURAL CONVECTION VENTILATION
EPDM ROOF MEMBRANE
1/2" CELOTEX
1/2" CDX PLYWOOD
6 MIL PLASTIC VAPOR BARRIER
CENTER OF COLUMNS
BASE LINE
8" DIAMETER WOOD COLUMN
6x6 POST BEYOND
FINISH FLOOR

Above - Interiors of a thermal mass building in
the
REACH Community in Taos, New Mexico
photo credits - Jonah Reynolds

Left - images of a "Hut" Earthship in the Greater World Community in Taos, New Mexico
Below and right - section and plan of an Earthship using the "U" shaped rooms and circular rooms.
Following - The shell house in Taos, New Mexico

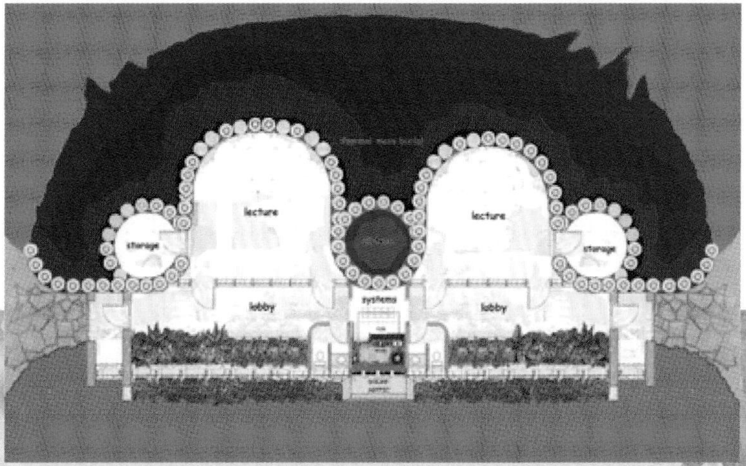

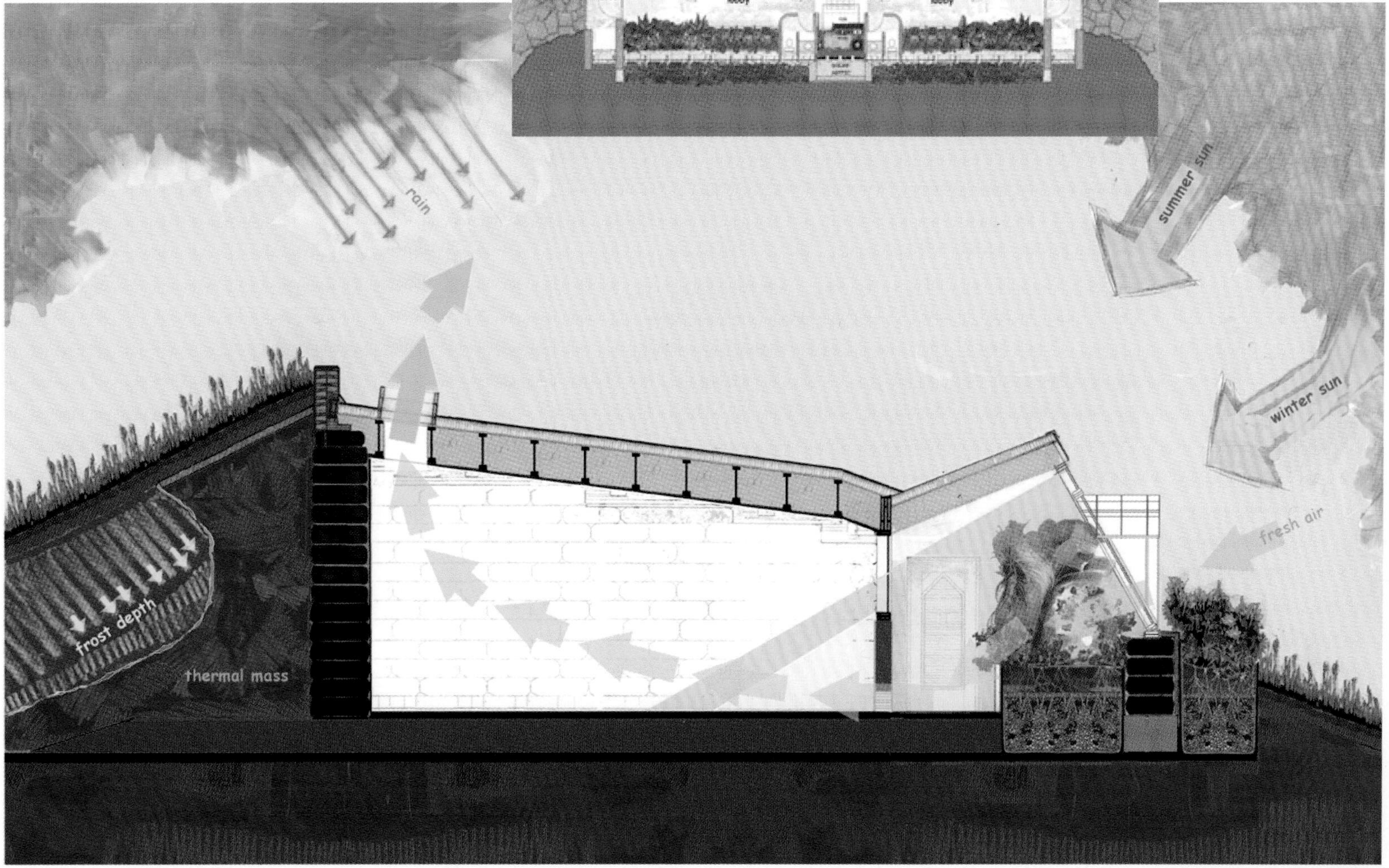

When comfort in any climate is learned...

we will no longer be looking through wires at dirty skies.